Novalis

UNC | COLLEGE OF ARTS AND SCIENCES
Germanic and Slavic Languages and Literatures

From 1949 to 2004, UNC Press and the UNC Department of Germanic & Slavic Languages and Literatures published the UNC Studies in the Germanic Languages and Literatures series. Monographs, anthologies, and critical editions in the series covered an array of topics including medieval and modern literature, theater, linguistics, philology, onomastics, and the history of ideas. Through the generous support of the National Endowment for the Humanities and the Andrew W. Mellon Foundation, books in the series have been reissued in new paperback and open access digital editions. For a complete list of books visit www.uncpress.org.

Novalis
German Poet—European Thinker—Christian Mystic
Second Edition

FREDERICK HIEBEL

UNC Studies in the Germanic Languages and Literatures
Number 10

Copyright © 1954

This work is licensed under a Creative Commons CC BY-NC-ND license. To view a copy of the license, visit http://creativecommons.org/licenses.

Suggested citation: Hiebel, Frederick. *Novalis: German Poet--European Thinker--Christian Mystic*. Chapel Hill: University of North Carolina Press, 1954. DOI: https://doi.org/10.5149/9781469657554_Hiebel

Library of Congress Cataloging-in-Publication Data
Names: Hiebel, Frederick.
Title: Novalis : German poet — European thinker — Christian mystic / by Frederick Hiebel.
Other titles: University of North Carolina Studies in the Germanic Languages and Literatures ; no. 10.
Description: Chapel Hill : University of North Carolina Press, [1954] Series: University of North Carolina Studies in the Germanic Languages and Literatures.
Identifiers: LCCN 54062201 | ISBN 978-0-8078-8810-0 (pbk: alk. paper) | ISBN 978-1-4696-5755-4 (ebook)
Subjects: Novalis, 1772-1801.
Classification: LCC PD25 .N6 NO. 10

TABLE OF CONTENTS

                                                                               Page

Preface ix
Introduction: Novalis, Then and Now 1

PART ONE

Life and Love

1. Beginnings 5
2. A Boy Goes Out to Meet the World 8
3. Schiller in Jena 11
4. The Tree of Knowledge 13
5. The Call of Destiny 16
6. Orpheus and Eurydice 18
7. The Diary of Death 24
8. At the Academy of Freiberg 27
9. The Rise of the Romantic Movement 30
10. Death, Herald of Life 34

PART TWO

The Works

1. Blütenstaub 38
2. Novalis and Goethe 41
3. Magic Idealism 49
4. The Novices of Sais 53
5. The Tale of Eros and Fable 59
6. The Hymns to the Night 68
7. Devotional Songs 78
8. Christendom or Europe 87
9. Heinrich von Ofterdingen 98
10. The Blue Flower 111

  I. Editions of Novalis' Works in the English Language 119
 II. Essays and Studies about Novalis and his age,
     published in the United States and Great Britain 119
III. Index. Persons and Places 123

PREFACE

Friedrich von Hardenberg (1772-1801), the leading poet of early German romanticism, is known the world over by his penname Novalis.

All his creative works were written within the short period of three years, namely between the late spring of 1797, when his beloved Sophia died, and the summer of 1800 when he fell mortally ill. Each of these years reveals a new facet of his creative genius. In the first year, we see the philosopher and natural scientist at work; in the second, the writer of beautiful fairytales, and finally the mystic poet of Christianity. Novalis died before he reached the age of twenty-nine.

His thousands of notations, which he called "literary seedlings," show the universality of his mind. The aphoristic nature of Novalis' literary legacy make difficult the presentation of a coherent picture of his life work. The presentation itself may, in spots, appear aphoristic. New vistas, deeper perspectives, reveal themselves at every step. His writings often afford glimpses at an ultimate synthesis, at a vast vision of the world as a whole. While synthesis and vision are not present in a completed form, they ever reveal themselves with the stimulating power of germination.

Up to the present, the writings of Novalis have been incompletely available in English translation and many of those existing are inadequate or outdated. Thomas Carlyle, in an essay published in 1829, first acquainted the English-speaking world with the German poet, translating a portion of the Fragments that were then available. The novel *Heinrich von Ofterdingen* was published in English translation by a member of the Harvard faculty under the title *Henry of Ofterdingen* (J. Owen, Cambridge, Mass. 1842, second edition H. H. Moore, New York 1853). An edition of the essay *Christendom or Europe* appeared in London in 1844, followed by *Hymns and Thoughts on Religion*, Edinburgh 1888. A much inferior version of *Novalis, His Life, Thoughts and Works* was compiled by M. J. Hope in Chicago 1891. Hope also translated the brief biography by Just, as well as numerous aphoristic thoughts and the lyric cycle *Hymns to the Night*. The *Geistliche Lieder*, in both German and English, were published in 1910 in Chicago, in a volume *The Devotional Songs*, edited by B. Pick. The fourth volume of Kuno Francke's *The German Classics*, New York 1913-1914, contained a translation of the fairy-tale *Hyacinth and Rosebud,* portions of the first two *Hymns to the Night,* one of the *Devotional Songs,* one *Song of Mary,* and a few aphorisms.

During the last decades there has been evidence of increasing interest in Novalis, particularly among the French surrealists. Besides various translations of his works into French, Spanish, Dutch and Russian, a new English translation of the *Hymns to the Night* by M. Cotterell (with an introductory essay by August Closs, Bristol University) appeared in London in 1948. Numerous aphorisms and poems translated into English were printed in various magazines, to mention only one—*Twice a Year,* double number XIV-XV, New York 1946/47. A new rendering of the *Novices of Sais* by Ralph Manheim, with a preface by Stephen Spender and with sixty illustrations by Paul Klee, was published by Curt Valentin in New York, 1949.

This present study is not a translation of the author's book *Novalis, der Dichter der blauen Blume,* A. Francke, Berne 1951 (361 pp.). It represents in structure and content a condensed version, adapted for the American reader. It is the first critical evaluation of the life and works of Novalis to be published in America, or any other English speaking country. It appears without scholarly apparatus. Scholars and students of the Germanic language and literature can avail themselves of the German book with its complete bibliography and extensive notes pertaining to the entire research on Novalis.

Moreover this monograph does not include any English verse-translations. In spite of some good translations, the thought content is so difficult and the versification so delicate that it seemed wiser to use the original German wherever the content made quotation necessary. The reader is referred to translations listed in the appendix, particularly to the new rendering of the *Hymns to the Night* (London 1948).

The author wishes here to express his deep appreciation for help on the part of Mr. H. Norden and Mr. Dean Howard who aided him greatly in preparing the English version of this study, and of Professors F. E. Coenen and B. Q. Morgan for their generous advice and friendly interest in the final process of its publication. The Research Council of Rutgers University has kindly facilitated the completing of the manuscript.

Wagner College F. H.
Staten Island, N. Y.

INTRODUCTION

Novalis, Then and Now

Today, more than 150 years after the death of Novalis, his spiritual stature has not stopped growing. From behind the historical personage born Friedrich von Hardenberg, there emerges with ever enhanced grandeur the unique creative personality who chose to call himself Novalis. The pseudonym had its roots in family history. In previous centuries several Hardenbergs had taken the cognomen "von Rode" (from the German verb *roden*, to clear land, latinized as "de Novali") from an estate named Grossenrode, near Noerten, in Hanover. The name thus seems to have meant "one who clears new land"—a pathfinder or pioneer.

The destiny and character of Novalis were bound up with the very fact of this symbolic pen-name. At the time of his premature death, his works were known to but a few of his friends in the Romantic movement, and the first edition of his writings, two slim volumes, appeared only a year later. Five further printings followed at intervals until the middle of the century. Not until the last third of the nineteenth century was Novalis rediscovered, and his international fame was not assured until the turn of the twentieth century.

Posterity has no portrait that does justice to his appearance in the years of his maturity—and this, too, is part of the symbolism of his life. In 1845, almost half a century after the death of the poet, Eduard von Buelow brought to Berlin and showed to the aged Ludwig Tieck a portrait he had found among the ancient furnishings of Oberwiederstedt castle. Tieck, the only surviving friend who had known Novalis in his youth, was asked whether the picture bore any resemblance to the long-dead friend. He acknowledged its authenticity, yet the old man must have keenly felt the inadequacy of this youthful portrait. Another likeness, also found in the possession of the Hardenberg family, again shows Novalis only as a youth, presumably before his twenty-first year.

Tieck himself, many years before, in the preface to the collected works he had edited with Friedrich Schlegel, had described Novalis at his prime: "Novalis was tall, slender and of noble proportions. He wore his light brown hair in locks that fell to his shoulders . . . His brown eyes were bright and luminous and his complexion, especially above the intellectual brow, was almost transparent... The set and expression of his features came very close to those of St. John the Evangelist, as shown on the fine, great tablet from the brush of Albrecht Dürer, which is preserved at Nuremberg and Munich.... Without the slightest vanity or intellectual arrogance, a stranger to all affectation and hypocrisy, he was a man in the truest sense, the finest and purest embodiment of a lofty, immortal spirit."

Novalis lived in an age when European idealism was in its glory. He was a few years younger than Hegel and Schleiermacher, Hölderlin and Beethoven; the same age as Friedrich Schlegel. He was senior by only a few years to Schelling, Tieck and Wackenroder. Soon after his birth the first performance of Goethe's *Götz von Berlichingen* shook the German stage, and the appearance of *The Sorrows of Young Werther* was a literary landmark in Europe. When Novalis was ten years old, Schiller's *The Robbers* heralded the coming of a new German Shakespeare. He read *Don Carlos* when he was still at intermediate school, and as a student in Jena he attended Schiller's lectures on history. He read Kant's *Critiques* when they were first published. The growth of his own mind was contemporary with the beginnings of Fichte, Schelling and Schleiermacher, all of them sunning themselves in the glory of the spirit of Goethe. As a boy he worshipped Bürger. Wieland, who printed his first verses in the *Merkur*, became his mentor when he was still almost a boy. He was Goethe's dinner guest, was welcomed in Schiller's house, and paid visits to Herder and Jean Paul. The Schlegels and the Tiecks, Dorothea and Caroline, Ritter and Steffens, all members of the Romanticist circle in Jena, were among his most intimate friends.

In a broader sense, his life encompassed the last perfection of Mozart, the mastery of Haydn, the titanic beginnings of Beethoven, the French Encyclopedists and their literature of the Enlightenment and, simultaneously, the beginnings of a new mysticism with Claude de Saint Martin and the Dutchman Hemsterhuis. The brief span of his life saw such events as the Declaration of Independence of the United States of America, the French Revolution, the beginnings of Napoleon, the invention of the lightning-rod by Benjamin Franklin, the discovery of galvanic electricity, the chemistry of Lavoisier, Priestley's discovery of oxygen, the invention of the steam engine...

Amid this confusion of a thousand voices only a truly great mind could find its own. In a time of so much stimulation and so many influences, the danger of mere imitation was ever present. Novalis, in ill health and facing the tragedy of early death, amid professional preoccupation and official trips, despite constant study and social intercourse, nevertheless in three brief years created a world that was wholly his own, a world that bears the stamp of his genius.

Friedrich Schleiermacher, the philosopher and theologian of the age of early German romanticism, wrote in the preface to his *Reden über die Religion:* "I shall refer you to ... that divine youth who too early fell asleep, to whom all that his spirit touched became immediately a great poem; and whom although he has hardly done more in fact than utter his first strains you must associate with the richest poets. In him behold the power of the inspiration and reflectiveness of a pious soul; and confess that when philosophers will be religious and seek God, like Spinoza, and artists will be pious and love Christ, like Novalis, then will the great resurrection be celebrated for both their worlds."

Not until a generation after his death did the eyes of the non-German world begin to focus on Novalis. Foreign research began with Thomas Carlyle's essay in 1829, in which the German poet was first introduced to the English-speaking world. This profound connoisseur of German literature, admirer, friend and translator of Goethe, wrote, that no student of literature can pass him by without attention. "Novalis, a man of the most indisputable talent, poetical and philosophical; whose opinions, extraordinary, nay altogether wild and baseless as they often appear, are not without a strict coherence in his own mind, and will lead any other mind that examines them faithfully into endless considerations; opening the strangest inquiries, new truths, or new possibilities of truth, a whole unexpected world of thought, where, whether for belief or denial, the deepest questions await us."

As a result of the influence of Carlyle's essay F. S. Stallknecht of Harvard translated the novel *Heinrich von Ofterdingen* in 1842 and remarked in his preface: "He (Novalis) resembles among late writers the sublime Dante alone, and like him sings to us an unfathomable mystical song, very different from that of many imitators, who think that they can assume and lay aside mysticism as they would a mere ornament."

M. J. Hope, who in 1891 published new translations (in an American edition) of many *Fragments,* the *Hymns to the Night, Heinrich von Ofterdingen,* and the brief biographical sketch by

Just, wrote: "Thinkers such as Pascal, Coleridge and Novalis, arise at intervals to rouse men's minds from their lazy acquiescence in the conventional. All who are not bound by the chains of dogma or prejudice, all who are real seekers after truth, must receive with gratitude these sparks and flashes of a deep-thinking spirit."

Maurice Maeterlinck introduced Novalis to the French-speaking world late in the nineteenth century. The great Belgian poet and mystic translated the *Novices of Sais* and many fragmentary thoughts (Bruxelles 1895), pronouncing these memorable words on him: "He does not torment himself. He never seeks himself in fear and trembling. He looks down on the scene below with gentle indifference. He gazes at the world with the inattentive curiosity of an idle angel, distracted by faraway memories."

In the middle of the nineteenth century Novalis and the other poets of German romanticism were sharply rejected by Heinrich Heine. Friedrich Hebbel called Novalis "a poetic nihilist," Heinrich Laube compared him with a bird of paradise "without feet, condemned to hover evermore in the air" and Franz Grillparzer spoke of a "Novalis deification of dilettantism."

Despite these attacks the *Devotional Songs* of Novalis were used in the Lutheran hymnals in Germany shortly after his death and gradually found their way into the hymnals of the Protestant churches all over the world. They appeared sometimes slightly changed and without the author's name as if they were common property or folk-songs.

Novalis' writings were revaluated by the philosopher Wilhelm Dilthey, who published an essay on Novalis (*Preussische Jahrbücher*, 1865) that is a landmark in the interpretation of the poet. It was subsequently incorporated into Dilthey's famous book *Das Erlebnis und die Dichtung*. It was thinkers like Dilthey and creative writers like Ricarda Huch and Maurice Maeterlinck who rediscovered the masked visage of Novalis. The first critical edition of his complete works, edited by Jacob Minor, appeared in 1907, to be superseded by the greatly expanded edition of *Novalis Schriften*, edited by Paul Kluckhohn in cooperation with Richard Samuel (Leipzig 1929). A multitude of German editions with partial translations into all cultural languages is to be found all over the world. Americans and Britons, Frenchmen and Belgians, Dutchmen and Danes, even a Chinaman with an excellent study, have joined hands with the scholars of the German speaking countries in an ever deepening appreciation of his works.

Part 1
Life and Love

1. BEGINNINGS

On May 2, 1772, a son—his first—was born to Baron Heinrich Ulrich Erasmus von Hardenberg at Oberwiederstedt castle in what was then the County of Mansfeld in the heart of Germany. The boy's name was entered in the baptismal register of the Lutheran church as Georg Friedrich Philipp. Rumors soon trickled beyond the walls of the family mansion that the child was sickly, dreamy-eyed and slow to develop.

Gloom filled the chamber of his birth in the chill castle apartments. The castle had been an adjunct to an ancient convent dating back to the thirteenth century. It had been in the Hardenberg family since the Thirty-Years' War. There was about it a legend of a walled-up gate. Once upon a time an ancestor, so went the story, had stood awaiting his bride at the main portal. The carriage had just rolled into the courtyard and the young woman was about to set foot on the threshold, when a sudden bolt of lightning killed her on the spot. Marking this dreadful stroke of fate, the lord of the manor had the main gate walled up and henceforth only a side-door gave entry to the building.

Thus the ancient family chronicle, with its legendary tale of love, marriage and death, of gloomy and foreboding destiny denied fulfillment. Whatever its truth, the main gate remained walled up indeed. Ancient trees formed a park, barren of flowers, that surrounded the massive Gothic walls which were dominated by a donjon. As for Friedrich von Hardenberg, the tragic legend of love and untimely death seemed to have struck a keynote that resounded in his life as though the theme were woven into the very fabric of his being.

Scion of an ancient family of Lower Saxony, going back to the Hohenstaufen dynasty and the War of the Minstrels at Wartburg castle, Friedrich von Hardenberg had inherited the rich cultural refinement of his ancestors together with the delicate constitution of later generations. Nine of his ten sisters and brothers died in infancy or early youth and only one brother survived his mother.

The ancestral seat of the clan was Nörten castle, the ruins of which still stand in southern Hanover. In the seventeenth century the family had split into two lines, one holding the title of count, the other that of baron. The former gave rise to a number of eminent diplomats and statesmen. The latter, to which the poet belonged, lived the quiet life of minor officialdom. The Counts of Hardenberg were steeped in the worldly traditions of the Age of Enlightenment and of rationalism. But the poet's branch of the family had embraced Pietism, that great mystical movement within German Protestantism. It was his father's mother who had first opened her heart to the Pietist doctrine and who had sought, at first in vain, to convert her son to the teachings of Spener and Zinzendorf.

In this son, the poet's father, the fateful story of love and death was enacted a second time. This time it is amply attested history rather than legend. In his youth and early manhood, father Erasmus had led a wordly life, in keeping with the Age of Enlightenment. Suddenly a plague of smallpox broke out among his villagers. His young wife was eager to care for the sick. But Hardenberg was overcome by fear and soon fled with her. His lady had been in perfect health. Scarcely had she escaped the precincts of Oberwiederstedt castle, however, when she died, a victim of the pox.

The inner change his Pietist mother had so devoutly desired now took hold of Erasmus. "After a wild and profligate life," he later said, "in 1769, on the occasion of a severe shock, the death of my wife, I began to feel a serious sense of disquiet about the state of my soul. The pious education given me by my late mother had inspired me, even in tender years, with principles that had left powerful impressions on my soul. God in his infinite patience had preserved these even amid the welter of vice to which I had so long surrendered."

The frivolity of the Rococo Age was banished, replaced by a Pietist devoutness that tyranized the Hardenberg family life with its dry austerity. Father Hardenberg entered into a solemn written compact with God which he renewed each time he took communion. He married Auguste Bernhardine von Bölzig, a poor orphan girl who had grown up in the Hardenberg household. She was a humble and dutiful wife who bore him eleven children. Their homelife was puritanical. Visitors were discouraged—there was to be no entertainment or diversion to disturb the sober order of the house. Devotions and bible lessons were governed by a precise daily routine. All too frequently the father's piety took the form of blustering pedantry. Tieck humorously tells of a visit he once paid to the house, during which he heard a scolding voice from an adjoining room. He asked a servant what had happened and was told: "The Master is holding religious instruction."

The first education which the sickly and dreamy-eyed boy received was given by a tutor. The Oberwiederstedt villagers were for the most part poor Mansfeld miners and thus private instruction for the children of the castle became a virtual necessity. The tutors were preachers or theology students from the Pietist community at Neudietendorf, situated between Erfurt and Gotha. As for young Friedrich, until his ninth year, the ordinary process of learning remained closed to him. The story goes that his younger brothers Erasmus and Anton easily outstripped their older schoolmate.

In the ninth year crisis came. For months dysentery confined the boy to his bed. Parents and physicians expected the worst. But Friedrich did not die. His cure was accompanied by a remarkable mental awakening. His ability to learn grew day by day. His memory became truer, his attention steadier, his gift of observation more powerful. Scarcely had he caught up with his younger brothers in his lessons when he began to outdistance his elder sister, and his tutor soon felt no longer equal to the demands of his headlong spirit. His father, therefore, decided to send the son to the fraternity of the church at Neudietendorf, hoping the boy might there be confirmed in the Pietistic traditions of his parental home.

When the boy, scarcely ten years old, arrived at Neudietendorf, Count Nikolaus Ludwig von Zinzendorf had been dead some twenty-two years. His figure had grown to legendary proportions, combining the features of reformer, revolutionary, and saint. Surely this must have had an effect on the inner life and imagination of the boy. In his lively fancies he must have envisioned Zinzendorf in America, founding his brotherhood at Bethlehem in Pennsylvania, receiving in the British colonies the same friendly support Wesley had given him in London.

Whatever the power of these impressions, the fact remains that the ten-year-old began to resist the orthodoxy of the Neudietendorf brotherhood. His tutors were quite unable to understand or guide him. His revolt against inherited forms of thought and living was manifest more in opposition to the mode of life than to the creed of Pietism.

When faced with the problem of bringing up his firstborn

son, his father despaired. His wife, after the premature delivery of her sixth child, had fallen seriously ill. Gloom deepened in the quiet home. The bitterest blow of all to the father was his son's refusal to stay at Neudietendorf until his confirmation. Finally a plan was agreed upon that seemed to hold out the best solution, though it was tantamount to surrender on the part of the father. It was decided to send the boy to his uncle at Lucklum in Brunswick.

2. A BOY GOES OUT TO MEET THE WORLD

Friedrich Wilhelm von Hardenberg, senior by many years to his brother Erasmus, was a Lord of the German Order of Knighthood and Knight Master of its Commandery of Saxony. He was a man of the world and lived a lordly bachelor's life on his rural estate at Lucklum, near Brunswick. In sharp contrast to the unworldly and unsociable spirit of Herrnhut Pietism that dominated the frugal mansion at Oberwiederstedt, the Hardenberg estate at Lucklum was the meeting-place of urbane aristocrats.

To the boy the visit to Lucklum brought acquaintance with an altogether different aspect of the life of his times. It was the Age of Enlightenment and of courtly absolution, over-ripe and weary, marked by etiquette and wit, elegance and fashion, irony and irreverence. Here in the library of his uncle—whom little Fritz and his brothers and sisters dubbed "Grand Cross"—the alert lad found works that could never have crossed the threshold of the mansion at Oberwiederstedt. There was Goethe's *Götz von Berlichingen* and *The Sorrows of Young Werther;* Wieland and Lessing, Shakespeare and Cervantes, and the books of the French Encyclopedists.

It would be hard to imagine a greater contrast than that between the Pietist community at Neudietendorf and the overblown late Rococo world of the rural estate at Lucklum. There were countless guests at the table—officers from Prussia, cousins from Göttingen, knights of the Order from the Electorate of Saxony. Unwittingly they drew the dreamy country-boy into the atmosphere of rationalist skepticism and the enlightenment, nourishing a tendency toward hot-house precocity. Within a year's time this state of affairs had become so apparent even to the uncle that he wrote his brother at Oberwiederstedt: "The tension in my house is pitched too high for his youthful head. He is becoming spoiled. I have too many visitors and cannot help it if there is much discussion at my table that is not good for him."

What the uncle envisioned for the boy was a proud career in the government service. He saw him as a future minister in the Saxon Cabinet, at the very least, and was concerned with molding the boy into a man of the world. Father Hardenberg, on the other hand, insisted on confirmation at the Neudietendorf community, desiring only to make him a Pietist. The uncle stressed fluency in the French language, the father in the catechism. The uncle cultivated the social graces of the rural aristocracy; the father banned all social intercourse, regarding it as sinful.

Under the impact of these conflicts the boy soon grew aware of himself as an individual and acquired a precocious independence of judgment. "His mind shows the culture, but also the limitations, of an aging man of the world," he once said about his uncle, and later he wrote his brother Erasmus about his father: "The Old Man and I simply are at loggerheads in our thinking and acting."

An incisive change in the family fortunes came when the boy was thirteen years old. In December 1784 his father was appointed, by the Elector of Saxony, supervisor of the salt works at Weissenfels, a state monopoly. The family left the lonely estate at Oberwiederstedt and moved to the pleasant little town on the river Saale. True, the father did not relinquish his puritanical bent, and his new residence at Weissenfels too was closed to all sociability, but the children soon found their friends beyond the confines of the home.

Even then young Friedrich's thirst for knowledge was all-encompassing. He promised his uncle a report on the French *L'histoire de Thou.* Of Steinbrecher, the justiciary at Schlöben, the family estate, he requested an Italian grammar and a catalogue of Italian books. At the behest of his friend Heimbach he read Young's "Night Thoughts" in German translation.

At the age of seventeen he sought to communicate with Gottfried August Bürger, his first approach to a contemporary German poet. His acquaintance with Bürger and the works of Wieland opened the door to the world of classical antiquity. In May 1789, barely seventeen, he paid a personal visit to Bürger at Langendorf. Soon afterward he sent his first verse to a publisher, under the pen-name of "Ensign von Hanstein." The poem, dedicated to Bürger, as yet lacked a note of its own. As he confessed to his Weissenfels friend, the publisher Severin, it was the fashion for "every youth to make rhymes, whether sad or merry."

Of most importance during this period of ferment was his approach to the world of antiquity. This meant another step toward independence, away from the Pietism and Puritanism of his home. He asked Christian Brachmann in Leipzig to get him the works of Euripides, Aeschylus, Theocritus, and many others. Rebelliously and at once yearningly his letter cries out: "You live in Athens-on-Pleisse (Leipzig), but we here on the banks of the Saale live as in Boeotia, far from the Muses and their temples."

At last the time came to leave the Weissenfels home, "far from the Muses," and to go to Eisleben to attend the upper classes of the *Gymnasium*, the traditional German high school. He lived in the home of Principal Jani, who himself taught the classical languages. As a member of the upper form of the Luther Gymnasium at Eisleben, he was wholly immersed in the study of antiquity.

There are fragments of a translation from Ariosto and of a sonnet to Petrarca that date back to the time of his Italian studies at Weissenfels. To these earlier efforts were now added a translation of the ninth canto of the Odyssey, fifty-five verses from the Iliad, Virgil's Eclogues, the Idylls of Theocritus, Pindar's Eleventh Olympic Ode and fragments of a few of the Odes of Horace.

It is quite true that all these translations and imitations were mere student exercises, revealing no poetic or linguistic originality. Yet it seems as though a deeper wisdom guided the immature hand as it leafed through the books, suddenly halting at certain places. Surely his pen must have tried itself on the famous Horatian Ode, *Quo me Bacche rapis tui plenum*. We know only the translation he made seven years later, in words dredged up from his very depths, neither imitative nor labored but welling from him with primal force, as though we were reading an ode from the best of Hölderlin or a fragment from Novalis' own *Hymns to the Night:* "Wohin ziehst du mich,/ Fülle meines Herzens,/ Gott des Rausches,/ Welche Wälder, welche Klüfte/ Durchstreif ich mit fremdem Mut/ . . . . Unerhörte, gewaltige/ Keinen sterblichen Lippen entfallene/ Dinge will ich sagen . . . /"

3. SCHILLER IN JENA

In the fall of 1790 Father Hardenberg sent Friedrich to Jena to study law, where as destiny would have it, he chose Schiller as a teacher and gained in him an elder friend. This occurred during the second year of Schiller's active professorship.

For the first time in his life he faced the living presence of genius. This time it was not the dim spirit of some dead reformer that moved the student, no pale shade of Virgil or Horace. Here was a great man in the flesh.

Hardenberg's acquaintance with the work of Schiller dated back to the time before he came to Jena. Probably in Eisleben if not before, he wrote his *Apology for Friedrich Schiller*, rejecting criticism of the latter's poem "Gods of Greece." This little article is of significance to a psychological understanding of Hardenberg's development. In it he takes to task the orthodox and narrowminded who had reproached Schiller with being an atheist.

The Schiller who now faced him was not the lyric and dramatic poet, but rather the philosopher and historian. Schiller's three-year study of Kant's philosophy lay just ahead of him. One of Schiller's colleagues was the philosopher Reinhold, whose courses on Kant exerted a wide influence. They were Hardenberg's first introduction to philosophical thought, an interest that was to become ever more strongly the guiding star of his creative work. He seemed to have worked hard as a student of Reinhold; however there is nothing in his letters to show that he became an ardent follower of Kant. On the contrary, like most of the creative and artistic minds of his time, he found that Kantian philosophy became a source of inner conflict. His correspondence with Reinhold revealed no reflections on Kant but contained long treatises on Schiller. There can be no doubt whatever that it was Schiller who was the crucial experience of his years at Jena.

The enthusiasm Hardenberg felt for Schiller was more than uncritical hero worship accorded him by hundreds of other students. To him Schiller was not merely an authority on history; he was the poet of philosophy, a creative artist concerning himself with history of the world, one of mankind's great teachers.

The studies of law enjoined by his father were actually not advanced at all during this year, which, instead, represented an ecstatic immersion in history and philosophy. At this time his first published verses were printed by Wieland in the *Teutscher Merkur,* a poem entitled "Plaint of a youth," signed only with his initials. Tone and rhythm are wholly those of Schiller. Poetically there is not a single element of originality. Stamped with Schiller's demand for self-discipline the little poem is still wholly under the spell of Kant's categorical imperative. An act must be done against one's inclination, in obedience to duty. Perhaps this poem already anticipates the mood that found such strong expressions a year later in Hardenberg's sudden decision to become a soldier.

We have a letter from the pen of Hardenberg's erstwhile tutor, addressed to Schiller at the behest of the father who had grown fretful over the neglected law studies. Schiller had already left Jena at the time, but it is quite likely that as a result he saw Hardenberg, either at Rudolstadt or Erfurt. For some time later Hardenberg confessed to Schiller: "You were the one who drew my attention to the more mundane purposes a sound head can and must choose here. Thus you supplied the final, decisive impetus which at once firmly fixed my intentions, at least," he added, "my affection for the dulcet arts of the muses will never die."

The father now decided to recall his son from Jena and send him instead to the University of Leipzig. Returned to his home in Weissenfels young Hardenberg addressed a letter to Schiller, vowing unswerving loyalty and assuring the poet that he would fight for him against all enemies with the "fiery zeal of Elijah." That fiery zeal sworn by a twenty-year-old never wholly vanished, even when Hardenberg allied himself in friendship with the early romanticists, with whom Schiller was destined to break later on.

The most intimate expression of his worship is contained in a long letter to Reinhold, a perfect essay on Schiller, whom he calls "one of these rare men to whom the gods have revealed face-to-face the lofty secret that beauty and truth are one and the same goddess; that reason alone is the name and the salvation given to man down here below, the only true logos, issuing from God and returning to him . . . . . I recognize him for the lofty genius who hovers over the centuries . . . . . the teacher of the century to come . . . . a citizen of the world whose heart beats for more than mankind."

4. THE TREE OF KNOWLEDGE

Hardenberg enrolled at the University of Leipzig together with his younger brother Erasmus whom the father had sent along in the hope that the two sons might pursue their law studies in rivalry with each other. Friedrich did indeed go to Leipzig with the firm resolve "to make it my strictest rule to fast my soul with respect to the arts," as he wrote to Reinhold in a farewell letter, "so that I may seek to gain more firmness, more resolution, more purpose, more planning."

"Destiny," a new friend soon reported, "has put a young man in my hands who bids fair to become everything. He pleased me mightily and I went out of my way to meet him. And soon he opened wide his heart's sanctuary to me, wherein I have now established myself to cast about."

The man who wrote these words in January 1792, to his brother August Wilhelm, was Friedrich Schlegel. Hardenberg and Schlegel, at the very first sight, had sensed their meeting to be a stroke of destiny. They were of almost the same age, Friedrich Schlegel but two months Hardenberg's senior. They bore the same Christian name. Of the same new generation, they had grown away from the twililght of the Enlightenment and the Rococo Age and had been thrust into the afterglow of the French Revolution and the dawn of German idealism.

The attraction was between opposites. Schlegel, intellectually precocious, was far superior to Hardenberg in critical judgment. He was a child of his time, tinged by skepticism and irony. Hardenberg, on the other hand, the pupil of Schiller, still was the pensive youth worshipping the ideals of beauty and moral law. Even then Schlegel was developing the journalistic gifts of the pamphleteer, the skilled polemicist, while Hardenberg was still concerned with sensitive lyrical nuances. Schlegel's judgment of art had already achieved a degree of sophistication, while Hardenberg displayed an innocent and artless enthusiasm.

That was why Friedrich Schlegel wrote to his elder brother August Wilhelm almost in a tone of condescension, though with deep admiration: "He is still a very young man, slender and well-formed, his fine face punctuated with dark eyes of commanding expression, especially when he talks spiritedly about the beautiful . . . . The study of philosophy has given him great facility in formulating fine philosophical thoughts. He is not pursuing truth but beauty. His favorite writers are Plato and

Hemsterhuis. On one of our first evenings he presented his views to me in fiery, almost savage fashion. 'There is no evil in the world,' he said. 'Everything is again approaching the Golden Age'."

Friedrich Schlegel was the first to have an inkling of the great lyric gift that still slumbered within Hardenberg. "He will be everything or nothing," he wrote, and two months later: "Hardenberg is rash to the point of wildness. He is always full of active, restless pleasure ... He does not yet know what to make of me."

Schlegel became Hardenberg's critical conscience. He called his friend's attention to "restless divagations" and "prolixity." He criticized the "superabundance of half-finished images." In long discussions he introduced his friend to his own social and political theories about the French Revolution, philosophized about and against Kant, talked about the latest literary productions. But perhaps of most importance was the fact that Schlegel slowly involved Hardenberg more deeply in the study of classical antiquity, leading him from his Apollonian admiration for Schiller's "Gods of Greece" to the Dionysiac aspect, the nocturnal and ecstatic dream world of Hellas. Schlegel, quite unconsciously himself still an apprentice, was even then laying the groundwork for the ideas associated with his own later romantic vision of Greece, which first found expression in his *History of Greek and Roman Poetry*.

The impulse for all of Schlegel's work stemmed from his demonic nature, which was proud and self-assertive, persuasive and commanding. His impact on Hardenberg was Mephistophelian, fascinatingly seductive with honeyed thoughts, chaotic but brilliant. It sought to supplant with irony or sentimentality the living pulse of true emotion, rooted in a deep and innate devoutness, such as Hardenberg possessed. Hardenberg fought against this self-righteous, cynical, and skeptical criticism, these heartless intellectual acrobatics. The relationship was marked by constant tension and vacillation: Hardenberg now drawing back in suspicion, now surrendering himself without reserve. Today he would be overwhelmed, tomorrow repelled. Nine months after their first encounter the tension was relieved. The situation had become intolerable. There was an open break.

"To be as truthful with him as I permitted myself to be, I should have had to engage in far more lies and flattery ... in the end injured vanity convinced him that my attitude was rooted in malicious fault-finding and insensate pride. He regarded me as indifferent and began to lose faith in me." Thus wrote Friedrich Schlegel to his brother in November 1792. He mentioned that the two friends had barely avoided a duel. "Thereafter," he added, "his trust died, as did my affection, forever."

But the crisis became the touchstone rather than the rupture of a friendship, for destiny seemed to have linked the two more deeply. Leipzig was still the same Little Paris which Goethe had left twenty-three years earlier, broken in health, his studies unfinished. For a time Hardenberg, too, seemed to succumb to its temptation. Names like Laura, Louise, Lotte and Lucy suddenly crop up in his verses and letters. Apparently both young men had unhappy love affairs. At any rate, the common experience of unrequited love completely reconciled the two friends. Hardenberg, moreover, got into debt, a fact that reached the ears of the University authorities.

In desperation, Hardenberg suddenly decided to give up his studies and become a soldier. It was an attempt to escape from his inner self. Three months before his twenty-first birthday he wrote a long letter to his father: "To become a soldier—that is now the utmost limit of my horizon and my desires .... I knew little about my own passionate nature. I never thought that anything like that could lay hold of me to my innermost soul ... I still must be educated. Perhaps I shall educate myself to the day of my death."

But the notion of becoming a cuirassier in the Elector's Guards proved illusory, when the revenue steward at Eisleben, to whom Father Hardenberg had sent Novalis, informed him of the family's straitened fortunes. This letter was still another disappointment to the father as it meant that Novalis' studies had again been disrupted. Brother Erasmus had fallen ill and had gone to visit his uncle at Lucklum. The sojourn at Leipzig became a mere episode for Hardenberg.

As he sat in the quiet of his Weissenfels home late in March 1793 reflecting on the past year in Leipzig, Hardenberg was quite aware of the disappointment he had been to his father. He had recently received a letter from Friedrich Schlegel with whom he was again on familiar terms. He answered at once: "Your eyes sparkle with supernatural fire. ... You will live as few men live, nor will you die an ordinary death, of course. You will die of eternity. You are her son and she will call you back. Yours will be rare destiny granted by God. Perhaps I shall never again see a man who is your equal. To me you have been the High Priest of Eleusis. Through you I have come to know heaven and hell, through you I have tasted of the Tree of Knowledge."

5. THE CALL OF DESTINY

Three weeks after his twenty-first birthday, Hardenberg matriculated at the University of Wittenberg. Wherever he turned he was treading in the footsteps of Luther. Here in one year and a quarter at the scene where Luther had once nailed his Ninety-five Theses at the door of the Court Church, Hardenberg at last completed his law studies. He also immersed himself in the study of ecclesiastical history. This study, against the background where Martin Luther had once set the world aflame for centuries to come, followed with inexorable logic Hardenberg's earlier interest in the philosophy of history. In the history of the Church he sought to trace the true evolution of Christianity, vaguely aware that only this evolution could reveal the true meaning of history.

In still another, narrower sense he seemed to be following Luther's footsteps. After the stormy eruption of his ego during the year at Leipzig with Friedrich Schlegel, the pendulum of his life swung back in the direction of tranquillity.

"It's a strange thing with both of us," he wrote his brother Erasmus. "At Leipzig we cut brilliant figures on the worldly stage. Now one of us is repenting at Wittenberg, cracking hard Latin nuts and sprinkling his hair with the dust of ancient tomes; while the other is suffering boredom in a backwoods hamlet among the natives ... I am much more thorough and worldly-wise than ever before. I am looking forward to the fall term and my examinations. This bourgeois life is delightful. All my extravagant youthful notions seem to sink down to the level of scheduled work."

He assured his father: "Work agrees with me, and as far as French is concerned I face the fall term with confidence. My hours are brimful with national and international law, statistics, and research. I am eager for an early appointment that will cut me loose from your pursestrings." To his mother he spoke of his "sense for a happy family life," adding that the family was closer to him than the state. "Only through my family am I directly bound to my fatherland."

It seems almost as though the world of Schlegel had become completely submerged in Hardenberg's soul. After a considerable time, in the summer of 1794, he received a letter from Schlegel again to which he replied (a month earlier he had passed his bar examination and had returned to Weissenfels): "I left Wittenberg suddenly, to enjoy my own company. I have had my fill of youthful turmoil. Here I shall await the call of my destiny with composure."

It was at Weissenfels that Hardenberg sought to regain his equilibrium between the two extremes of Leipzig and Wittenberg. Thus we find the strange conflict within him still unresolved. "My life is complete even now," he cried out, yet he concluded with the following profession of faith in Schlegel: "Mark well that I shall become and remain worthy of you. Our paths must come closer and closer until we both catch fire from a single flame."

He was waiting with composure for the call of his destiny, yet he confessed that his life was complete even now. To the outward view this "complete" life appeared as that of an average talented cultivated young man from an ancient family of the German nobility that traditionally supplied candidates for officialdom. Neither the poems that appeared in Wieland's *Merkur,* nor the early efforts under the influence of Matthison, Hölthy, Bürger, Gleim, and Klopstock revealed a voice that was truly his own. He was inescapably an emulator of Schiller.

Some time before, Schlegel, disturbed by the manner in which Hardenberg scattered his studies, had mentioned his friend's "extreme heedlessness' to his brother. Hardenberg dabbled in history without becoming a historian; he pursued mathematics without system; his scientific interests were casual. His studies in ecclesiastical history occupied but odd hours in secret during his two final semesters. He passed his terminal law examination only by dint of "cramming."

Deep into Hardenberg's twenty-third year, nothing revealed the stamp of genius. Even in his correspondence his style followed contemporary taste. One of his letters to Reinhold reads like an undergraduate thesis in philosophy. He imitated Schiller's hymnal pathos. His exchanges with Schlegel were tinged with the emotionalism of Werther. To his family he wrote in conventional domestic style.

It was in this mood that he arrived at the little town of Tennstedt on October 25, 1794. He had been engaged as a law clerk to the District Justiciary, Just, in whose house he lived. At once he threw himself into the practice of official correspondence and reports. Coelestin Just, twenty-two years his senior, was soon singing the praises of his youthful apprentice, crediting him with great zeal and accuracy.

Work took up three-fourths of the day, but in the evening he may have read the first essays of Schlegel, just published—*The Schools of Greek Poetry* and *Women Characters in the Greek Poets*, soon to be followed by a third, *Diotima*. It was those essays with which Friedrich Schlegel embarked upon his literary career, making his mark on the German public scene years ahead of Hardenberg.

Hardenberg pursued his studies in his remote and quiet nook. He may have read the *Women Characters* about mid-November, perhaps even *Diotima*. Was he awaiting his destiny "with composure" and without forebodings?

On November 17 he started out on an official journey, in company with his senior associate. They were to levy taxes at Grüningen Castle. A ride of two hours and a quarter took him to the estate of Cavalry Captain von Rockenthien.

He saw Sophia von Kühn. The hour of destiny had struck.

6. ORPHEUS AND EURYDICE

The relationship with Sophia von Kühn and the events that took place henceforth in Hardenberg's life cannot be readily understood in terms of conventional standards. Laboriously compiled biographical details add up to little more than anecdote, skirting the trivial on the one hand, the pathological on the other —a sentimental episode of bucolic dalliance.

"In a quarter-hour my mind was made up," Hardenberg insisted to his brother Erasmus. How could such a remark be taken seriously at the time? Sophia was not yet thirteen years old, her womanhood unawakened, a school child who had difficulty with her spelling, naively and uncertainly putting down her words as they were pronounced in the dialect of Saxony. She was ten years younger than Hardenberg. She had grown up against the gusty background of the happy-go-lucky military gentry, amid blustering hunting parties and drinking bouts staged by her stepfather, Captain von Rockenthien, surrounded by a flock of exuberant brothers and sisters, sheltered by a French governess, Jeannette Danscour.

The spontaneity of her sunny, childlike nature and the grace of her presence enthralled Hardenberg from the first moment, but they do not explain the awakening of his soul and the consecration of his spirit that sprang from their meeting and gave focus to his whole life. He loved as he had never loved before. Affections such as he had felt for Augusta Jani had been no more than passing schoolboy fancy. His relationship with a certain Julie at Leipzig had been a student escapade. His verses to various Minnies and Carolines at Jena and Wittenberg had only skimmed the surface of a youthful temperament in an age of emotionalism. Even his attachments to married women older than himself, such as he had experienced at Weissenfels, were no more than fleeting way-stations. He had made fun of them himself and broke them with repentent irony.

It is impossible to believe that his soul had ever before been touched by such inexorable faith in the destiny of love such as Sophia's which overwhelmed his whole being and all his senses.

All at once he was aware of it. "What birth denied me, good fortune has given into my hands. In my own family circle I missed what I see gathered in this company, so strange to me. I feel that there are affinities closer than blood." These words were addressed, not to Sophia, but to her stepsister, Wilhelmine von Thümmel, almost thirty years old. His sincere attachment to Wilhelmine, seven years his senior, seems no less strange than the circumstance that Jeannette Danscour often took care of Sophia's correspondence or herself added postscripts, or that he addressed the governess as though she were one and the same person as Sophia. Even down to the final period of their official engagement, the two lovers never relinquished the formal style of addressing each other to the more familiar form.

The first note Sophia scribbled to him with spelling mistakes reads as follows: "Lieber Hardenberg, Erstlich danke ich Ihnen recht sehr für Ihren Brief, zweidens für Ihre Hare und dritens für das niedlichste Etwie welges mir sehr fihlen Spas gemacht hatt. Sie fragen mich ob Sie an mich schreiben dürfen? Sie können versichert sein dass es mir allemahl sehr angenehm ist von ihnen einen Brief zu lesen. Sie wissen lieber Hardenberg ich darf nicht lange schreiben. Sophia von Kühn."

This letter conveys the motivation, tone, and attitude of all the other notes, messages, slips of paper and postscripts that passed from Sophia to Hardenberg. They all have the same schoolgirl diction and spelling errors, the childlike pleasure over little gifts of locks of hair or vanity cases, the conventional and almost cool statement that she is glad to receive letters, the formal address using only the name Hardenberg, and finally the recurrent mention of her bodily weakness, her ailment, her suffering—"I must not write long letters." Initially she signed her letters with her full name. This was shortened to Sophia and finally Sophie, but style and contents showed no material change or growing maturity.

To Hardenberg Grüningen was paradise. When dating letters written there he sometimes called it "Elysium", though he was not unmindful of the slippery jokes of the down-to-earth cavalry captain that formed the "dark and dirty side," as he called it. On Sophia's thirteenth birthday the two plighted their troth in secret, but about the middle of the next year there seems to have been a jealous spat, with indications that Hardenberg had been too friendly to a certain Jette von Goldacker. But soon Jeannette Danscour, the go-between, assured him "I see many signs that our little Sophia is by no means indifferent to you and that her sole pride is to see you beloved and esteemed of all men."

Her stepfather once limned Sophia in a letter to Hardenberg, shortly after she first fell ill: "Sophia dances, gambols, sings, sleeps like a top, walks as straight as a ramrod, is merry and full of fun, has had her fill of whey and drugs and everything, is scheduled to take two more bath treatments, and for the rest is as sound as a fish in the pond."

Sophia on her part, in a little note, again asked Hardenberg for a lock of hair: "The other day I wanted to look for it but neither hare nor papper were there and now I beg you once againe be shorn, naimely your head. Sophia von Kühn."

Hardenberg's vision of her is laid down in a diary passage headed "Clarissa: Her precocity. She wishes to please all. Her obedience and her fear of her father. Her decency and yet her innocent trustfulness.... She does not wish to be anything. She is somebody.... She can make little of poetry.... She does not seem to have reached the stage of actual reflection... It is her wish that I shine wherever I go. She resented that I addressed myself to her parents too soon, and that I let it be known too quickly and too generally. She likes to hear stories. She does not want to be put ill at ease by my love. My love often weighs heavily on her. She is thoroughly cold... She does not believe in a life to come, but does believe in the transmigration of souls."

Elsewhere he called Sophia Sakuntala, and only a year after the first meeting, when she fell ill, he idealized her as the incarnation of philosophy.

Sophia's first serious illness came in November 1795, a year after the first encounter with Hardenberg. Soon after this period his love and devotion seemed redoubled. On Sophia's fourteenth birthday, when she had scarcely recovered, the engagement was announced to the family circle at Grüningen. In July, 1796 the disease erupted anew and Sophie lay at the point of death following an operation at Jena. It was at this time that Hardenberg sought the consent of his own father as well. During these summer weeks and months, while Sophia suffered agonies in the clinic of Court Councilor Starke at Jena and the first sorrows and forebodings of death overshadowed the youthful happiness, Hardenberg's love first seemed to flame into true ecstasy. It grew as Sophia's body wasted away. It fed on the ever rising uncertainty of her recovery, and came to full flowering in the face of her final ordeal and slow extinction.

Four days after her fifteenth birthday Sophia died. Hardenberg henceforth began to seek her in the underworld of his soul. Her death became the rebirth of his spirit. The trifling world of the late Rococo sank away. Fluttering preoccupation turned to brooding melancholy as his scattered interests gave way to contemplative calm. His being had found its focus. The earthly name of the departed bride fused with the symbol of the heavenly Sophia and gave birth to the mystery of love by which Friedrich von Hardenberg became the poet Novalis.

This love, so fleetingly rooted in mortal life, yet engraving its mark forever in the life of the spirit, has often been likened to Dante's love for Beatrice. "Every beloved object is the core of a paradise," Novalis wrote, and this is true of Sophia as it is of Beatrice. The Eternal Feminine in both women drew their lovers onward into the world of the spirit and behind Dante's inward road, as behind Novalis' stands the same prototype, the prototype of the poet himself, as projected in its most human and beautiful version in the Greek myth of Orpheus and Eurydice.

It is Orpheus, who was the first of the bards, and his love for Eurydice that manifests the archetype of the mission of poetry. As the son of Apollo and the muse Calliope his lyre had the power to move the rocks and tame the savage beasts—the power of ennobling nature through the harmony of man. The nymph

Eurydice, to whom he was bound by destiny and love, was his muse, his higher self. But the sting of an adder suddenly tore her from her beloved and she vanished into the realm of shadows. Orpheus descended to the underworld to bring her back. Guilt and tragedy joined into destiny. By turning to glance at Eurydice while he was still in the underworld, Orpheus transgressed the law of Hades and thus she vanished a second time. What was left to him was the power of his song, the vision with which he knew himself linked to the world of the dead, whose herald he became. He lost Eurydice in the mortal world, but won his independence. His descent into Hades gave him the wisdom of accepting death.

The descent to the nether world became the orphic archetype of the poet's way. It is from this aspect that we must understand the tradition that made Orpheus the ancestor of Homer and Hesiod. For the core of the Odyssey too is the descent to the underworld by which alone the hero can find his way back to Penelope. Virgil too has Aeneas descend to the realm of the dead before he reaches his goal—and it is Virgil who mentions the myth of Orpheus and Eurydice in his *Georgica*, as do Ovid and Horace in their fashion.

Orpheus's descent to the nether regions, during which he won Hades and Persephone over to his side, assuaged the Eumenides, calmed the Judge of the Dead, and overpowered Cerberus, while the Parcae ceased their spinning of the thread of fate and Charon left his boat—all this was a familiar topic of pre-Christian paganism.

In the Christian era the descent to the underworld becomes transformed into the path of salvation, directed upward. Dante's companion in the Inferno and Purgatory is Virgil, as the last descendant of Orpheus. But Beatrice, not the pagan Virgil, is the guide in Paradise. From the *Vita Nuova* we know about Dante's encounter with the nine-year old child, his second meeting with the eighteen-year old girl, and the powerful vision of her spiritual figure which he experienced after the early death of his beloved.

When Beatrice Portinari died, Dante was twenty-five years old. And Novalis was at precisely the same age when he suffered the death of Sophia von Kühn. A mysterious parallel seems to have determined the destiny of these two Orphic Christians. For both of them love was kindled by a child destined to die young. For both of them death became the occasion for poetic consecration, a "new life." Both were overwhelmed and guided by visions and ultimately inspired to the transfiguration of their beloved. At the age of twenty-eight Dante finished the last sonnets in the *Vita Nuova*, which ends on a note of promise—the promise of the *Divina Commedia* as the supreme apotheosis of Beatrice. At the same age Novalis finished his *Hymns to the Night*, had them published and wrote at his *Heinrich von Ofterdingen*, the second unfinished part of which promised the ultimate apotheosis of Sophia. For both poets the bride of their soul became the queen of heaven, the epitome of Paradise joining them to Christ. Yet neither of them escaped the demands of the physical world and of mortal love. For, two years after the death of Beatrice, Dante married Gemma Donati; and two years after Sophia's death Novalis was betrothed to Julie von Charpentier.

Certainly these noteworthy parallels must mark certain common traits of destiny, yet they contribute nothing to a final understanding of these individuals. For Dante and Novalis are as different from each other, as incomparable, as are Homer and Virgil, or Virgil and Dante. Behind Dante stood the undivided Latin-speaking universe of the Gothic middle ages, of scholasticism and mysticism. Confronting Novalis was a socially disorganized Europe, divided into many small states, rent by religious strife, the Enlightenment, the French Revolution, and soon to be engulfed in the Napoleonic wars. On the one hand was the Gothic Age at its prime, on the other the age of the late Baroque. Here was the dogma of the indivisible World Church, there ecclesiastical schisms and sectarianism with all their consequences. Here fullness of the spirit, there nihilism of the faith. Here the cathedral as the symbol of communion, there individualism driven to its heights of isolation. Behind Dante rose the framework of the *Summa Theologica* of Thomas Aquinas, while the spirit of Novalis developed against the background of Fichte's philosophy of the ego. Thus the love of Sophia consecrating Novalis as a poet remains a unique event, utterly individual in character.

When he heard of the girl's illness, even Goethe visited Sophia von Kühn as she lay in the clinic at Jena. He told how deeply moved he was at the sight of her innocent suffering. On the Good Friday following Sophia's death—the same day on which Novalis' brother Erasmus prematurely succumbed to a lung ailment inherent in the family—the young poet, surrounded by the me-

mentos of threefold death, wrote to Woltmann at Jena: "I shall not conceal from you that I could not regard him (Goethe) as the apostle of beauty, had he not been moved at the very sight of her. Surely it is not passion. It is too inexorable, too cold, too deeply rooted in my very soul—this feeling that she is one of the noblest, idealest figures ever to walk the earth."

7. THE DIARY OF DEATH

Novalis' diary is dated by the death of Sophia, beginning the Tuesday following Easter, shortly after the impact of Good Friday and the death of his younger brother. Not until May 2, his twenty-fifth birthday and six weeks after Sophia's death, does Novalis appear to have visited her grave at Grüningen for the first time. These were weeks of confusion and weakness, fluctuating between hope and despair, composure and anxiety, confidence and utter abandonment. He stood before a great void. It was the kind of ordeal of the soul, hovering between suicide and insanity, to which both Kleist and Hölderlin succumbed, but from which Novalis emerged more and more victoriously as he became certain of his spiritual image of Sophia.

"My love has become a flame that slowly consumes all that is earthly. Your hope has been borne out. There are within my soul more powers of healing, of endurance and resistance, than I myself had known. It is a healing power that stifles the evil at its source." Thus he wrote to Friedrich Schlegel; and to Woltmann: "My powers have waxed rather than waned. I often feel now that it is meet that this be so. I am wholly content. I have gained anew the power that rises above death. My being has taken on unity and form. Even now a new inner life is burgeoning within me."

Thoughts of suicide and yearnings for death rise to the surface again and again, as seen in his correspondence with Friedrich Schlegel, who as long ago as their first meeting at Leipzig had toyed with the notion of suicide by poison. On May 13, Schlegel seems to have sent Novalis a copy of Shakespeare's *Romeo and Juliet* and *A Midsummer Night's Dream*. The translation was taken from the pen of his brother August Wilhelm, and the book had not yet been placed on sale. In this respect there is a significant passage in Novalis' diary, describing another visit to Sophia's grave, a passage that in some respects anticipates the language of the third "Hymn to the Night," and that is of fundamental importance to his inner development: "I rose at five o'clock in the morning. The weather was very fair. The morning passed without my doing much work. Captain Rockenthien and his sister-in-law and children came. I got a letter from Schlegel with the first part of the new Shakespeare translations .... I began to read Shakespeare and got really into it. In the evening I visited Sophia. I was indescribably happy there. There were flashes of ecstasy. I wafted the grave before me as though it were dust. Centuries passed by in a flash. Her presence was tangible—I felt she might appear at any moment. . . . Later in the evening some good ideas came to me. Shakespeare gave me much food for thought."

At no other point of his life could Shakespeare's classic tragedy of love have had a more powerful effect on the unhappy and bereaved Novalis. He read a passage such as that when Romeo breaks open Juliet's tomb and drinks poison in her presence:

> Ah, dear Juliet
> Why art thou yet so fair? Shall I believe
> That unsubstantial death is amorous;
> And that the lean abhorred monster keeps
> Thee here in dark to be his paramour?
> For fear of that I still will stay with thee,
> And never from this palace of dim night
> Depart again.
> (Act V, Scene 3)

This Romeo mood prevailed for several days and seemed to grow stronger, for the next day there is an entry that repeats the sentiments of the preceding day: "Last night I visited the grave and had a few moments of wild joy." But his Romeo fever made him add: "In the evening everyone soon went to bed, I still conversing with Mrs. Mandelsloh alone, about Sophia and myself. The decision has often been discussed these days. I am still troubled by my mother and father, and by the method. There has been much thought of Sophia; nor was there even now any lack of frivolous thoughts."

The "decision", "method", and the "frivolous thoughts" doubtless refer to his notion of committing suicide, a notion enhanced by the reading of *Romeo and Juliet*. Two days later we again find: "Afterward I read Shakspeare. Then I went to the dear picture closet, unlocked the cabinet, looked at the things that belonged to my Sophia, read my letters and her whole supply of correspondence. Afterward I was all with her. . . . Then back to the grave. The day was very fair, but the evening was not to my liking, though the decision received new life, new firmness." The next day he was "anxious at the thought of Sophia. . . . I was not moved at the grave. The decision was vivid. It is only that I must live more and more for her sake. I exist only for her, not for myself or anyone else. She is the highest, the only thing. . . ."

So the days passed. He observed "sensual stirrings" in himself, "much lustfulness," "little emotion at her grave," "anxiety over her death," "the dreadful fact of her loss," and he spoke time and again of his "decision." On May 25 he had sent the Shakespeare translations back to Friedrich Schlegel with the following words: "Here is your Shakespeare. . . . It is curious that you should have sent me *Romeo and Juliet* just now. I have read it often. There is a deep meaning in what you say, that there is more than poetry here. I now have an inkling of what makes Shakespeare so unique. Surely he had his measure of the gift of vision. . . . I enjoyed the play just as it is. I am not yet able to make plain much of what I feel. The plot is magnificent— the ancient feud resolved in immolation and atonement—savage hatred dissolved in consuming love."

Henceforth the tone changes. "I must make a determined effort and learn to maintain my better self against the shifting scenes of life, changes in the mind. Ceaseless thought about myself and the things I learn and do." A reading of Fichte's *Natural Law* seemed to support this trend toward self-discipline and growing intellectual strength.

On May 29 he noted down an experience of great significance to him that took place while traveling from Tennstedt to Grüningen: "On the way to Grüningen it was my joy to grasp the true meaning of Fichte's Ego." This concept of Fichte's "Ego" struck him like a flash of intuition at the very spot where he had once, coming from Tennstedt, first seen the yellow battlements of Grüningen castle that were to be the scene of his meeting with Sophia.

Sophia's death had fallen during Lent. About Easter he himself had felt as though he were to follow in death. Between Easter and Whitsuntide he struggled with the temptation of suicide. Soon after that ordeal he had confessed significantly: "What I feel for Sophia is not love but religion. Absolute love, independent of the heart—love founded in faith—such love is religion."

A single lapidary phrase heads the diary entry for June 30,

which marks the end of such soliloquies. The words rise like a guiding star on his destined way:

"Christ and Sophia."

8. AT THE ACADEMY OF FREIBERG

On December 1, 1797, in the ninth month after Sophia's death, Novalis arrived at Freiberg in Saxonia to study at the renowned mining academy until Whitsuntide 1799. This study had become necessary if, as his father proposed, he was to be appointed to the staff of the Weissenfels salt works upon graduation.

His flight from the world, his despair and his yearnings for death were things of the past. His diary of death with its monologues of mourning transformed itself to his "continuing soliloquy," the writing of his hundreds of fragmentary thoughts. While writing his philosophical aphorisms he dedicated himself to the practical life.

The Freiberg period opened up the study of the natural sciences with an undercurrent of alchemy and theosophy. "If only we could meet," he wrote to Friedrich Schlegel, "to exchange papers with each other! You would find much theosophy and alchemy." Concerning his philosophical thoughts he had told his friend even earlier: "They are fragments of the continuing soliloquy within me, sinkers, so to speak."

The more he ventured into the recesses of his own mind, the more openly he surrendered himself to the world. En route to Freiberg he made the acquaintance of Schelling. Soon afterward he came to know the Körner family, friends of Schiller at Dresden. Later he visited Goethe at Weimar, in company with August Wilhelm Schlegel, and in Leipzig he met Jean Paul. In the summer of 1798 he went to Bad Teplitz to take advantage of the bath, then joined the Schlegel brothers, Schelling, Hülsen, Gries, and Böttiger at Dresden for companionable visits to the art galleries. Charlotte Ernst, Schlegel's sister, became a warm friend of his, and he spent many happy hours with the family of his cousin, Dietrich von Miltitz, at Siebeneichen castle near Meissen.

At the mining academy he threw himself into the study of nature, under the guidance of the famous geologist Abraham Gottlob Werner. He had scarcely arrived at Freiberg, when he was warmly welcomed into the home of Inspector of Mines Charpentier. A year later he became engaged to the daughter, Julie von Charpentier.

It is significant that during this very fall and winter, when he became engaged to Julie, Novalis wrote his first purely creative work *The Novices at Sais*, which included the lovely fairy tale of *Hyacinth and Rosebud*. Just as the great Florentine, bursting from the shackles after the death of Beatrice, began to find himself and to write his *Vita Nuova*, so did Novalis, at virtually the same age, begin to give form to his inner rebirth, his "new life," in poetic terms.

On January 20, 1799, Novalis confided to Schlegel that he had become secretly engaged to Julie, a fact not even his family at Weissenfels had learned. He communicated the news in words that are of great psychological interest. Note the passive mood in which the verb "love" is employed: "The relationship of which I told you has become closer and more binding. I see myself loved in a way in which I have never been loved before. The destiny of a girl exceedingly worth loving hangs on my decision. .... A most interesting life seems to await me. Nonetheless," he continued surprisingly, "to tell the truth, I were rather dead." The relationship with Julie did not seem to impinge at all on the sphere where Sophia dwelt. Love for Julia grew under precisely diametrical auspices. With Sophia Novalis had actively taken the initiative, to the company of an outburst of creative concentration and awakening. But the lonely recluse at Freiberg seems almost to have been driven into the Charpentier home, to have fallen under the spell of Julie rather than to have actively wooed her. Compassion played a greater part than love. Fear of solitude, the urge for a settled household, seem to have been more powerful motives at this time than all the memories of the grave at Grüningen.

He told Caroline Schlegel too about the engagement of which his father was still ignorant, relating Julie's miraculous recovery from long illness—on Christmas Eve her agonizing pain had suddenly dropped away: "For two months all that is part of the creative mind has been faltering within me. In all this long time I have not had three good ideas," he confessed significantly. "I now live wholly in the world of technology. My apprenticeship is moving to an end, and settled life with its varied demands is coming ever closer."

Friends around him published book upon book (about this

time there appeared *Lucinda,* the much-debated and decried novel by Friedrich Schlegel). Nothing had appeared from his pen except the aphoristic *Blütenstaub* in the *Athenaeum,* and *Faith and Love,* another collection of his aphoristic thoughts, in the *Prussian Annals.* Was he ever to emerge from the fragmentary state? Even his *Novices at Sais* was a novel of fragments rather than the fragment of a novel.

At Freiberg Novalis himself was still the "Novice" in each and every respect, a learner in the most universal sense and with the most intensive dedication. His devotion to work was praised as altogether extraordinary by all who knew him at this time. He alone, in true modesty, looked on it as a matter of course. As a student he took part in the living pulse of the immediate present. Werner's theory of the origin of the earth was at the time an epochal event. Ritter, one of Novalis' most beloved teachers, was himself a disciple of Galvani, the discoverer of animal electricity. Novalis pursued the study of chemistry under a student of the famous Lavoisier. When he found the lectures of the mathematics instructor too tedious, he sought the study of higher mathematics by a private tutor. His mathematical fragments show such originality that to this day students of his life attribute to him pioneer work in this field.

He integrated chemistry and medicine, mathematics and physics, psychology and physiology with his studies to the same degree as esthetics and linguistics, philosophy and history. Deep into the night he read Hemsterhuis and Plotinus, Spinoza and Plato. He knew several passages from *Wilhelm Meister* almost word for word. He read Goethe's *Hermann and Dorothea* and Schelling's *World Soul.* As a mining expert, he descended deep into the bowels of the earth, often spending more hours of the day below ground than above. Here too he was like an Orpheus visiting the underworld, an Apprentice at Sais, seeking to lift the veil of Mother Nature.

Thus he led a double life. He descended into the deepest shafts of the earthly world, while rising in his imagination into the highest realms. Betrothed to Julie, he composed the apotheosis of Sophia. He yearned for settled position and household, yet confessed to his friend, "to tell the truth, I were rather dead." He spoke of living "wholly in the world of technology," and all the while his desk held plans and notes for *Heinrich von Ofterdingen* and the *Hymns to the Night,* dedicated to the transfiguration of his immortal beloved.

It was the twenty-eighth year, which he entered when he had returned from Freiberg to Weissenfels, that was to bring the crucial turn toward maturity. In the mundane sense, the student at the mining academy became an assistant in the management of the salt works. In the poetic sense, the apprentice became a master.

9. THE RISE OF THE ROMANTIC MOVEMENT

In the life of Novalis we encounter a curiously delayed maturity, suddenly attaining a fulfillment such as has been vouchsafed to but few creative spirits. Heretofore all had been but planning. Now the building began. Heretofore only seedlings had been set out. Now they burgeoned into bloom and fruit. But this flowering was to be tragically brief. One full summer, a fertile fall, a busy winter, another spring, the anxious beginnings of one more summer—these were all that were to be granted him in his prime, before the final breakdown caught up with him, wracking him with painful inactivity.

It was the crucial meeting with Ludwig Tieck on July 17, 1799, at Jena, which made Novalis emerge from the stage of stagnation he had so clearly observed within himself.

Jena at the turn of the century! August Wilhelm Schlegel dwelt there with his wife Caroline, and at their table the friends met and "symphilosophized." Friedrich Schlegel and Dorothea joined them during September of this year. Schelling was lecturing for his second year at the University, the successor of Fichte. Johann Wilhelm Ritter was another member of the faculty. Henrik Steffens, natural philosopher from Norway, joined the Jena circle, and even Goethe came from nearby Weimar, often for days, sometimes for weeks and months. Within scarcely a decade the little town on the river Saale became one of Europe's cultural centers, like a Florence of the early Renaissance, suddenly becoming the birthplace of early German romanticism.

Gotthilf Heinrich Schubert, who journeyed to Jena on foot to study with Ritter, in describing the town tells how he was unable to resist wandering "over to the mountain, from which the castle ruins with the Fox Tower are visible far into the valley. ... The slopes of the bare ridges now seemed as though clothed in purple-blue velvet and green gossamer silk, for it was the time when the pasqueflower opens its great, deep purple blossoms, their infinite number transforming the rocky soil into a flower garden."

Of a summer day, against the background of such a countryside, Novalis met Tieck at the home of August Wilhelm Schlegel. By midnight the two were clinking glasses to seal their friendship. By the light of the full moon they wandered out into the night of the hills of Jena. It was a mutual inner awakening that took place.

"The acquaintance with you starts a new leaf in my life. I find joined in you so many things I have heretofore found but scattered among my acquaintances. Just as my Julie seems to me to possess the best of all, so do you seem to touch everyone in the flowering, to be my kin ... No one has yet stimulated me so gently and at once so universally. I understand completely each word from your lips." Those were the terms in which Novalis addressed his new friend. Tieck entered his life about the twenty-eighth year, as Friedrich Schlegel had done about the twenty-first. In Tieck, however, Novalis did not see the "High Priest of Eleusis" who taught him to eat of the Tree of Knowledge, but the herald of Jacob Boehme. In Tieck he found not the art critic and philosopher of culture, but the poet of "Franz Sternbald" and the friend of Wackenroder, the "art-loving monastic friar."

Tieck was a year younger than Novalis, but with incredible precocity he had written his *Almansur* at sixteen, *Abdallah* at eighteen, *Karl von Berneck* at nineteen. His *Story of William Lovell* appeared when he was scarcely twenty-three. *Peter Leberecht* followed soon afterward; and at twenty-five he published with certain additions of his own, the work of his contemporary and friend, Wilhelm Heinrich Wackenroder, *Outpourings from the Heart of an Art-Loving Monastic Friar*. Wackenroder had died in February 1798, and Tieck must have loved him like a twin brother. He resurrected his friend in the main character of his novel, *The Wanderings of Franz Sternbald*. Both Wackenroder and Sternbald revolved about a single sun. Its name was Raphael. To both of them Raphael was, as it were, the prototype of the fine arts in Italy, and Italy meant to them the Rome of the Renaissance, and the Renaissance was Raphael.

With the intuitive vision of true friendship, Tieck divined the spiritual background of themes in Novalis' "Hyacinth and Rosebud," in the "Apprentices," and in Klingsor's tale, from which later grew, in organic fashion, the *Hymns to the Night,* the *Devotional Songs* and the *Songs of Mary.* Unconsciously at first, and then more and more consciously, Tieck felt as though something of Raphael's Florence and Rome had reawakened, had, in the early Romantic Movement, become transformed from image to word. In the fall of this same year, Novalis read him his *Devotional Songs,* while Tieck and his wife were paying an extended visit to the home of August Wilhelm Schlegel. Tieck at once welcomed them as though a deep poetic dream of his very own had seen fulfillment.

During this period in the life of Novalis another thinker became his favorite philosopher: Friedrich Schleiermacher. Reading Schleiermacher's *On Religion—Discourses to the Educated Among Its Contemners,* and his *Monologues,* which appeared the following year, 1800—both of them made a profound impression on Novalis—one is often surprised at the fraternal similarity with which whole thoughts and sentences are set down, as though they had been conceived simultaneously. One remembers certain "Bible" fragments written by Novalis in the Freiberg period when one reads in Schleiermacher's "Discourses": "What is inspiration? It is merely the religious term for freedom. Every act of free will turning into a religious deed, every delineation of a religious view . . . is a matter of inspiration. . . . indeed, he who sees no miracles of his own from his vantage point in contemplating the world, within whom revelations can never rise . . . who does not sense that a divine spirit urges him on, that he speaks from sacred inspiration . . . who does not grow aware that his feelings are the immediate outgrowths of the universe. . . . that man has no religion."

"Every man is a priest," Schleiermacher proclaimed, "to the degree that he draws others unto himself and into the field he has staked out as his own." Such thoughts inspired Novalis as they burst upon him during this very summer and fall of 1799, when Tieck helped to resurrect within him the poet whose vocation Novalis had never wanted to see sundered from that of the priest and the seer. Without realizing the inspiring influence of Schleiermacher, much of what Novalis created and perfected during this time cannot be understood. Without ever having met, Novalis and Schleiermacher were brothers in spirit, at once speaking a common primordial speech with different tongues.

Tieck was the friend who supplanted Friedrich Schlegel at this time, and the world of Schleiermacher took the place of that of

Fichte. In the same way, it was the mysticism of Jacob Boehme that crowded out Hemsterhuis, who so long had held the Freiberg student under his spell. Even before the time of his friendship with Tieck, Novalis had read Boehme. This is shown clearly in his notes. But Tieck taught him to read Boehme in a new light.

"I am now reading Jacob Boehme in a greater content, and I am beginning to understand him as he must be understood. Throughout one sees in him the mighty power of spring with its burgeoning, growing and intermingling forces—forces that give birth to the world from within." At this time some of the works of Boehme had been translated into French by Claude de Saint Martin. They had long since appeared in England and the Netherlands. In Germany proper they had been in constant circulation, though the Age of Enlightenment and rationalism were utterly hostile to them. The onset of early Romanticism was linked as a matter of course with a renaissance of the world of Jacob Boehme. Among all the mystics none placed the mystery of the virgin Sophia as radiantly at the heart of Novalis' thinking as did Boehme.

In reviewing these fleeting days of Early German Romanticism at Jena, how did his friends see Novalis in retrospect?

Tieck wrote (in the preface of an edition of Novalis' writings in 1813): "His talk was animated and loud, his gestures bold. I never saw him fatigued. Even when we talked deep into the night, he merely broke off arbitrarily, to rest, only to read even then before falling asleep. He never knew boredom, even in the most oppressive company of mediocrities. . . . he liked best to reveal the depths of the mind in conversation, to speak with fervor of invisible worlds, yet he was as merry as a child, loved to make innocent jokes himself and readily surrendered himself to the jokes of others."

"I have seen Hardenberg," Henrietta Mendelssohn wrote to Dorothea Schlegel, "and I must begin by telling you about it, for I can think of nothing more interesting. He arrived here this noon . . . His fine figure, his transfigured eyes, his charm and friendliness in all matters are truly enchanting . . . . Hardenberg has electrified me."

"You must see him," Dorothea reported to Schleiermacher. "Even if you read thirty books of his you will not understand him as well as you will if you once take tea with him."

Henrik Steffens sketched the following picture in his memoirs: "On first impression his appearance recalled those devout Christians whose nature is simplicity itself. His clothes seemed to support this first impression, for they were quite plain, giving no hint of his noble lineage.... His deep-seated eyes, above all, carried an ethereal fire. He was wholly the poet... Novalis always seemed to speak as well as to write from a deep sense of the past, from an originiality of the spirit that found difficulty in expressing itself in terms of the active present.... Few men have left such a deep and lasting impression on me."

Novalis encountered little resistance. The only adversaries among former friends were Schelling and Caroline. The contrast between Novalis' and Schelling's philosophy of nature was rooted in the general outlook of the two men. Schelling's approach to nature was essentially intellectual and necessarily opposed to the intuitive response to nature of Novalis, the poet. Novalis posited a constant process of approximation to the infinite in nature, an "arch-infinitism," while Schelling always spoke of polarity ("arch-duality") as the fundamental law of nature.

In the midst of all of his studies Novalis was no bookworm or recluse. After the repose of the Freiberg years, he deliberately and joyously turned to the outside world. The office of the Weissenfels salt works was his headquarters. But official journeys demanded considerable traveling. He traveled to Artern at the Kyffhäuser Mountain, Kösen, and Dürrenberg. He would hasten to Julie at Freiberg, visit Reichardt at Giebichenstein in company with Tieck, go to Halle and Dresden, to Upper Lusatia and to pay a call to relatives at Siebeneichen Castle, near Meissen. At Weimar he again saw Jean Paul whose acquaintance he had made the year before at Leipzig. Four days after his first meeting with Tieck, they were Goethe's dinner guests again, along with the older Schlegel.

During all this time of movement and company, of hurried journeys and busy official preoccupation, Novalis prepared his *Hymns to the Night* for publication in the *Athenäum*, wrote his *Devotional Songs*, his essay *Christendom or Europe*, and was at work with his last project of greatest scope, the novel *Heinrich von Ofterdingen*.

10. DEATH, HERALD OF LIFE

Goaded by an inexhaustible imagination, Novalis conceived soaring plans for work to come. *Heinrich von Ofterdingen* was to be but one in a series of seven novels.... Plots concerning the

Reformation, the time of Paracelsus, the discovery of America, the crusades, the destruction of Constantinople followed on the heels of plans for "historical plays embracing entire nations, indeed, world history . . . a romantic book on the seasons . . . Prometheus, the dethronement of Saturn. Empedocles. Sappho. Aëtius. Constantine. Julian. The Last Judgment . . . A history of Christianity. . . . The destruction of Jerusalem. . . ."

During his work on the second part of *Heinrich von Ofterdingen*, on the wings of his imagination, he still had both feet firmly planted in his professional life. He descended into the bowels of the earth, making its law, its reality, his own. Five days after finishing the first part of *Heinrich von Ofterdingen*, he prepared a petition applying for a post as district justiciary in Thuringia. He proposed to take on these duties in addition to his responsibilities in the salt works and to establish a household of his own with Julie von Charpentier.

Professional work and social life vied for his time during the period when his deepest thoughts were concerned with the completion of his novel. In April he met his poet friends at Jena and again visited Herder and Jean Paul at Weimar; in May he inspected the alum works at Hohenelba, in the company of Just; Until mid-June he was on a mineralogical excursion through Thuringia. Around St. John's Day Tieck visited him at Weissenfels, and in a letter to Friedrich Schlegel he reported that the second part of his novel would be "far more poetic than the first, even in form," for "poetry has now come to life." About this time he went off on another official trip and again visited Artern at the foot of the Kyffhäuser mountain. . . .

On a single day in early August he composed no less than six more additional petitions to further his candidacy as district justiciary. He sent them to the Elector of Saxony, the Chief of Cabinet, two Ministers and two Councilors. He actually went to Dresden on the matter, but soon he was again at his office in the Weissenfels salt works.

Summer was in its prime—the fruits ripening in the sweetness of their juices, the grapes of the Saale valley drawing their last richness from the sun before the frosty fall would reach out its blighting hand—when the awesome flash of a hemorrhage rocked his body to its foundations, tearing open his delicate tissues, hurling him into the feverish pit of that disease that was his heritage—tuberculosis.

Seven months of bedridden suffering were to be his lot—weeks in which he victoriously wrested with fear and despair, tested himself in patience, rallied in divine faith, rose to saintliness in prayer and contemplation.

The final pages in his diary he called "an apprenticeship in the higher art of living, a study in the shaping of the mind." In ever-lasting self-observation he watched over the stirrings of his soul. "Oh that I were blessed with the sense of martyrdom," he exclaimed to himself. A question in his voice, he confessed: "Have I not from time immemorial chosen all my own destinies?" In the end he yielded to the resolve "to accept all that happens with a joyful heart as God's benison." In contrast to the diary of lamentation over Sophia, the yearning for death now gives way time and again to the will to live, the hope for recovery. Filled with this confidence, he dispatched to Dresden his test thesis for the post of district justiciary. A month later his younger brother Bernhard drowned in the waters of the Saale river. The news utterly prostrated him. Another hemorrhage made the doctors abandon hope of his recovery. From November until mid-January he lay in Dresden, "Scarcely a shadow," as Charlotte Ernst described him to her brother Wilhelm Schlegel, "no longer recognizable. . . . He seldom takes part in the conversation, merely listens—he has trouble speaking. Often he falls asleep and then he looks like one dead."

In the midst of this ordeal came the news of his appointment as district justiciary! Late in January he was returned to the parental home, still holding fast to his hope. He reported to Just that he was having trouble writing, but that he could again read, think, and take part in things. . . .

This is his last letter that has come down to us. On the fourth anniversary of Sophia's death he began to fail perceptibly. His cousin Carlowitz hastened to his side to see him once more, as did Friedrich Schlegel, faithful friend and witness in the hour of death.

Early in the morning of March 25, 1801, he asked for some books. Later on he took breakfast, and toward nine o'clock in the morning he asked his brother Carl to play for him on the piano. He listened to the music for a while, then gently fell asleep without another word. The sun rose toward its zenith when sleep beckoned him from his dream of music into the realm of night, the praises of which he had sung with such fervor.

He knew: "Life is the beginning of death. Life is for the sake of death. Death is the end and at once a beginning." Destiny had vested the poet with a new life after the death of his beloved, and now that new life had prepared a very special death for him. The death of this life was his last poem. It was a death that did not spring from the despair of a Kleist, in suicide inexorably indicting an indifferent world. It was a death triumphantly eluding the clutches of madness that unstrung the gentle lyre of Hölderlin.

The tragedy of his death was that his whole life-work was to be but a fragment. The fragment, however, was a seed-corn that fell on fruitful soil. The mortal body called by the name of Friedrich von Hardenberg crumbled into dust. But the work that went out into the world under the self-chosen name of Novalis still carries the message: "In death was germ of life eternal found"—the words of the bard from Hellas in the fifth "Hymn to the Night," where the poet already saw himself in mythical perspective.

Part 2
The Works

1. BLÜTENSTAUB

With the writing of his aphorisms Novalis began his creative work, regarding his fragmentary thoughts as "literary seedlings." That is why he called them *Blütenstaub (Blossom Dust)* Signed with his poetic cognomen of Novalis and published in the first issue of the *Athenaeum*, the aphorisms were indeed the most spontaneous expression of a new generation, destined to become the poetic youth movement of the early Romanticists.

In sketchy form they outlined the development of German romanticism. Kant's agnosticism is declared invalid. The inward realm of the self is without limitation of knowledge. Priest and poet again become one, as they were in the beginning, for "language is the dynamic element of the spiritual realm," and poetry aims at the union of man with the divine, because "the world of man is the common organ of the gods."

These fragmentary flashes of insight matured slowly from the lament of death. It was "the art of transforming everything into Sophia," and it marked the starting-point of the way in which the thinker was to become the poet, the poet in turn the seer. "When I believe that Sophia is about me and may appear, and while I act in keeping with this faith, she is about me indeed and at last surely does appear to me—in precisely the place where I thought I was myself, within me." In the end he said: "I have a beloved, Sophia—Philo-Sophia is her name."

For him philosophy was the altar on which poetry received the consecration of priesthood. "Bards and priests were one and the same in the beginning. Only later ages have sundered them. The true poet is always a priest, just as the true priest has always remained a poet." Philosophical thinking guarded him against the danger of trailing off into mere emotionalism and brought him clarity, knowledge, balance and self-discipline. Philosophy was not an object for his analysis but rather a synthesis of knowledge, faith and vision. "Symphilosophizing" is what the romanticists around him called it, this inward activity of the mind that recognizes no line between specialties, instead joining and permeating both history and science, ethics and chemistry.

aesthetics and physiology, mysticism and mathematics, philology and physics.

It was this philosophizing in the guise of his "beloved Sophia" that allowed Novalis to find himself again. Here in *Blütenstaub* the former notes of lamenting and mourning began to develop a diary of a mystic. Thus it contains notations such as this: "Life is the beginning of death. Life is for the sake of death. Death is the end and at once a beginning."

To be sure, his philosophical studies of Kant and Fichte began in Tennstedt even before Sophia's death. His notebooks are full of excerpts and comments on Kant's tables of categories, Fichte's epistemology, the writings of Hemsterhuis, Dumas, Simon, and Lessing. Many of these jottings are bodily taken over from other writers. The significant element in these preliminary studies is the gradual liberation from Kantian doctrines. He scored the Kantian method as one-sided and scholastic. "According to Kant," he wrote, "pure mathematics and pure science refer to the forms of outward sensibility. What science then refers to the forms of inward sensibility? Is there such a thing as extraordinary knowledge? Is there another way open of going beyond ourselves, of reaching other beings, of being affected by them?"

The first attempts to answer these questions appeared in *Blütenstaub* and the next collection of fragmentary thoughts, which he published in the *Prussian Annals* under the title *Faith and Love*.

Today it is true that one cannot read many of the sentences of *Faith and Love* without reservation. To be sure, some thoughts can easily be misinterpreted. Novalis called his second collection of fragments "grave mystic political philosophema," written in a "tropic and enigmatic tongue, understood but by him who ought to understand." These "political" thoughts have nothing to do with plain politics or patriotism. Novalis' concern is with a state of the future, a state of everlasting peace, when "all men shall fuse like a pair of lovers." These eschatological ideas of an ideal state were directly influenced by Schiller's *Letters on the Aesthetical Education of Man* (Letter IV) in which he wrote: "It may be urged that every individual man carries within himself, at least in his adaptation and destination, a purely ideal man. The great problem of his existence is to bring all the incessant changes of his outer life into conformity with the unchanging unity of this ideal. This pure ideal man, which makes itself known more or less clearly in every subject, is represented by the state, which is the objective and, so to speak, canonical form in which the manifold differences of the subjects strive to unite. Now two ways present themselves to the thought, in which the man of time can agree with the man of idea, and there are also two ways in which the state can maintain itself in individuals. One of these ways is when the pure ideal man subdues the empirical man, and the state suppresses the individual, or again when the individual *becomes* the state, and the man of time is *ennobled* to the man of idea." (Works of F. Schiller, Cambridge edition, Vol. VIII, Boston 1884, p.40.)

Thus Novalis' ideas concerning state or nation are always connected with ideals of education of man. In this realm he remained the faithful disciple of Schiller. Note the commentary of Novalis to his *Blütenstaub*. There are Germans everywhere. Germandom is no more limited to a specific state than Romandom, Greekdom, or Britaindom. They are general human types that have become dominant here or there; Germandom is independent of geography."

The following passage from the collection of fragments of the same year may further serve to clear up the question of Novalis' view of nationalism. It also had a deep affinity with passages of the fourth letter, *On the Aesthetical Education*, where Schiller speaks of the savage and the barbarian in contrast to the cultivated man: "Man can be opposed to himself in a twofold manner; either as a savage when his feelings rule over his principles; or as a barbarian, when his principles destroy his feelings. . . . The cultivated man makes nature his friend." In a similar manner Novalis wrote: "There are three main aggregations of mankind: savages, civilized barbarians, Europeans. The European is as high above the German as is the German above the Saxon, the Saxon above the citizen of Leipzig. Above the European stands the citizen of the world. All that is national, temporal, local, individual can be universalized and thus canonized and made general. Christ is a compatriot ennobled in such fashion."

It must be remembered that all these words were written long before the Napoleonic wars, the nationalist upsurge and the Wars of Liberation. Novalis wrote his aphorisms in the form of a fable of ideal man to come. To Schiller's aesthetic state he lent the symbolic name "Prince". "A true Prince is the artist of artists; that is to say, the master of artists. Every man should be an artist." Hence every man carries within himself the potential ideal of the "Prince."

His ever-recurrent poetic image of the Golden Age is the realization of Schiller's ideal state, as expressed particularly at the end of the *Letters on the Aesthetical Education of Man* (Letter XXVII). "Wherever there are children, there is the Golden Age," Novalis wrote in *Blütenstaub* and went on: "The lore of the fable holds the history of the primal world. It encompasses the past, the present and the future."

The Golden Age is Paradise Regained, when the childlike and at once divine element within man begins to awaken in the Biblical sense of the words: "Except ye be converted, and become as little children, ye shall not enter into the kingdom of heaven." (Matthew 18:3.) It is the praise of this "Child-nature" that Novalis sang. For him, it became source and wellspring to the writing of new fables.

2. NOVALIS AND GOETHE

"The Goethean Treatment of Science—a project of mine," thus Novalis noted in the collection of fragments he called *The General Brouillon*. It was not merely the author of *Wilhelm Meister* and the *Fairytale* who exerted a crucial influence on him, it was Goethe the scientist as well, the founder of a new botany and theory of color, the geologist and zoologist, the comparative anatomist and meteorologist.

Novalis was among the very first to recognize the significance of Goethe's natural scientific writings, although they had scarcely been published, with the exception of the little book *An Attempt to Explain the Metamorphosis of Plants* (which Goethe had had printed by a small Erfurt publisher in 1790, after Göschen at Leipzig had rejected it), and of his *Beiträge zur Optik*, 1792-93. Novalis, therefore, was a pioneer when he proclaimed prophetically: "His observations on light and on the metamorphosis of plants and insects are confirmation and at once the most telling proof that even purely instructive discourse belongs into the realm of the creative artist. In a certain sense one may rightly assert that Goethe is the first physicist of his time and has, in fact, made history in the field of physics. . . . Goethe, the physicist, occupies the same position with respect to other physicists as does Goethe, the poet, to other poets. In volume, diversity, and depth he may be exceeded here and there but who is there to equal him in creative power? With him all is action, as with others all is merely trend."

His characterization of Goethe's world outlook was carried even further. Novalis observed with unique precision Goethe's imagination, reason and power of abstract thought. In Goethe's intellect, "the gift of abstraction is seen in a new light. He never abstracts without at the same time constructing the object to which his abstraction corresponds. This is no more than applied philosophy, and thus in the end, not surprisingly, we see him as the practical, applied philosopher—something every true artist has always been."

This power of abstract thought combined with creative synthesis marks Goethe's method of apperceptive judgment, as he himself described it in an essay published in 1820, almost a generation after Novalis' remarks.

In Goethe Novalis saw the perfect and indivisible union of art and science. Here, too, he was a pioneer, for another century was to elapse before the identity between the poet and the scientist in Goethe began to be grasped. "The Goethean philosopher or thinker—Freedom grows with the culture and readiness of the thinker. The poet is but the highest stage of the thinker.... The division between poet and thinker is only on the surface—and redounds to the disadvantage of both." These are among his notes referring to Goethe.

To represent Novalis as no more than a Goethe imitator and enthusiast, to track down poetic influence and resemblances—nothing could be less conducive to an understanding of these two great minds. On the contrary, at the very time when Novalis was devoting himself to the study of Goethe in unreserved admiration, we see how he consciously contrived to maintain his integrity and aloofness. "Goethe will and must be outdistanced, but only as the ancients can be outdistanced, in content and power, in diversity and depth, not really as an artist, or at least but little. For the truth and discipline within him are perhaps even more exemplary than they seem."

Unintentionally Novalis here poses for himself and his poet friends of the early Romantic period the task of creating something by way of "content, power, diversity, and depth" that will not run counter to Goethe but rather will be capable of being carried into the future together with Goethe. In the affinity and contrast of these two minds it is possible to observe the primal phenomenon of two intellectual trends that were to become cause and source of the Romantic movement.

The parallels between the growth and development of these two poets are tangible facts. Both were powerfully affected by Pietism. Goethe at Frankfurt through Susanne von Klettenberg and her circle, Novalis through his family and education. Both attended the same University of Leipzig, failing there to complete the study of law. To both, Leipzig, the Little Paris, became a tempting backdrop for a worldly life, and both faced the task of surmounting the Rococo dalliance of the Age of Enlightenment. Both found in Herder and Lavater leaders for their minds and intellects. Alchemy, theosophy and the natural science of centuries past enriched both poets, and both took up the study of nature in a professional sense.

To questing man the world is revealed on a twofold level, outwardly and inwardly. His eye, looking out, envisions space, and experiences light as a phenomenon in space. But inwardly man lives the rhythm of time, senses word and tone within his ear. Light and tone, color and word, space and time, form and music, perception of eye and ear—these are the polarities of knowledge of the world and of self, the archetypal contrasts of Apollo and Dionysus.

Goethe's vision sought the light. His eye was turned outward in Apollonian fashion. His theory of light and color became the deepest expression of this mentality. On the subject of self-knowledge, however, he uttered these characteristic words: "I shall here acknowledge that I have always looked with suspicion on the grandiloquent injunction: Know Thyself. It seems to me a ruse on the part of priests secretly in league with one another, for the purpose of confusing man with unattainable demands, of leading him away from activity directed toward the outside world to a false inner contemplation. Man knows but himself insofar as he knows the world, for he sees the world but in himself, and himself in it alone."

At opposite poles from this Novalis wrote: "Language is the dynamic element of the spiritual realm," and, succinctly: "(Grammar)—language is Delphi." Language is Delphi—that means, it points the way toward self-knowledge, toward the "Know Thyself" graven into the porch of the Temple of Delphi. "Inward leads the mysterious way. Within us, or nowhere, lies eternity with its worlds, the past and the future. The outside world is a world of shadows—it casts the shadows into the realm of light."

Here Novalis puts the self-knowledge, the value of which was so doubtful to Goethe, at the very head of his creative work. This is why Novalis felt himself a priest of the word while he looked on Goethe as king in the contemplation of nature. This is why the poems of Novalis are at bottom devotional songs, while Goethe was worldly in the broadest sense of the word, a world poet for a world literature. Novalis proceeds from the self to the world. To him the highest task of self-education is "to be the ego's ego." Goethe, on the other hand, recognizes that the world sees itself in man, "rejoicing in the summit of its growth." That is why Goethe saw "God in nature, nature in God," while Novalis felt the divine within his own self-assurance, for conscience "is the innate mediator of every man. It takes the place of God on earth."

To Goethe religion was the fruit of the perfect union between science and art, and in his *Xenia Tamed* he said: "He who possesses science and art has religion as well." Goethe's religious experience was the fruit of his work, coming at the end of his road, a gift conferred by the wisdom of his old age. With Novalis religious experience, coincident with the death of Sophia, directed his early steps. For Sophia, who became his "beloved Philo-Sophia," he felt "not love but religion."

To Goethe philosophy, mathematics, and music were worlds that could move him only at the periphery of his own world outlook. To Novalis they were starting points and guiding stars for his inner orientation. Goethe evaded the world of Kant, Novalis overcame it. Goethe was a realist and was happy when his thinking was called objective. Novalis built a magic idealism of his own.

Goethe bestowed the bounty of his many completed works as full, ripe fruit, whereas Novalis scattered a thousand humble, hidden seedlings which he himself did not expect to see bear fruit.

Goethe roamed the ridges of the Thuringian forest, the Harz mountains, the Erzgebirge, tapping the rocks, watching the clouds. Novalis descended with the miners into their shafts and sought to grasp chemistry and halurgy, the nature of the "salt of the earth." His destiny led him ever deeper into the nocturnal side of nature, while Goethe watched sunlight in its variety refracted in the prism, seeing "colors as the deeds and passions of light."

Novalis' powers of judgment steadily grew and changed; his criticism as well as his praise and recognition were, in part, divinatory. In 1798 (in the *General Brouillon*) he passed this judgement on Goethe's *Wilhelm Meister:* "The philosophy and morality of the novel are romantic. Common, or uncommon, each element is seen and represented with romantic irony. The accents are melodious rather than logical, which is precisely what gives rise to such marvelous romantic order." Two years later (on February 1, 1800) he wrote: "Opposed to 'Wilhelm Meister's Apprenticeship.' At bottom it is a fatuous and silly book—pretentious and precious—unpoetical to the highest degree as far as the spirit is concerned." He called it a "satire on poetry and religion," a "knighted novel," "a pilgrimage to a patent of nobility," "actually a 'Candide' directed against poetry."

He began by praising Goethe's novel for its philosophical and moral character, describing it as romantic—which surely must be regarded as the highest praise. But soon afterward he fought it as a silly, fatuous, unpoetic book. To be sure, his original judgment was that of an impressionable disciple, his later verdict that of the poet of *Heinrich von Ofterdingen* at the peak of his maturity. But was he in a position to know Goethe, as we see the whole of him today? He had no acquaintance whatever with such works as the Easter scene in the first part of *Faust,* or the Helena scene, which were written in these very years. Indeed he actually seems to challenge Goethe to continue *Wilhelm Meister,* as was done decades later in *Wilhelm Meister's Wanderings,* the moral and religious profundity of which would surely have moved Novalis—to say nothing of the *West-Eastern Divan* and the *Orphic Orisons,* the studies on morphology and the second part of *Faust.*

Precisely because he once called Goethe the "vicar of the poetic spirit on earth" and the "first physicist of his age," we must take his verdict on *Wilhelm Meister* as being directed, not against the poet, but only against the novel. For at the very time when he raised the reproach of artistic atheism against Goethe, he also called him the "Boehme of Weimar." Surely this was the highest praise Novalis, fired with enthusiasm for the mystic of Görlitz, could have found for Goethe's view of nature.

It is noteworthy too that in the later writings of Novalis not a single word is to be found that calls into question his enthusiastic interpretation and reception of Goethe's *Fairytale*. On the contrary, the work inspired him to create his very own.

Goethe's *Fairytale*, which concludes his *Tales of the German Refugees* and first appeared in Schiller's magazine *Horen* in October 1795, was greeted with the greatest enthusiasm by all the Romanticists. August Wilhelm Schlegel called it "the fairest tale that ever fell from the heavens (of fantasy) upon the desolate earth." From the very outset it has challenged interpretation, and down to the present day we have had hundreds of expositions. But Novalis was the first to delve into its meaning and to show in his poetic work its immediate influence.

He approached Goethe's *Fairytale* in four different ways and at four definite points in time, all in the same year of 1798, when he was studying at the mining academy in Freiberg, and coming in touch with the same cultural background that influenced the scientific work of Goethe.

It does not appear to be mere chance that the first attempts to interpret this tale fell at the time immediately before or after the first visit Novalis paid to Goethe's house on March 29, 1798, with August Wilhelm Schlegel. Three direct meetings with Goethe are authenticated. This first visit was followed by a second, on July 21, 1799, when Novalis was Goethe's dinner guest with August Wilhelm Schlegel and Tieck; and a third, when he met the poet at a social gathering on November 14, 1799.

The first remarks concerning the *Fairytale* are found in a new collection of aphorisms which Novalis called *Poesy*. He later crossed them out in the manuscript, evidently because they did not seem to him to be mature enough for publication. Whatever the reasons for the deletion may have been, the sentences that follow take us directly into the workshop of his mind. Novalis was writing about the essence and mission of poetry in general, then adding a remark about Goethe's *Fairytale:* "Poetry is the great art of constructing transcendental health. The poet, therefore, is the transcendental physician. Poetry . . . mixes everything for its great purpose of all purposes—*the exaltation of man above himself.* . . . Heretofore poetry has for the most part had a dynamic effect. The transcendental poetry to come may well be called organic." Novalis then explained form and content of the drama as "a process of transmutation, purification, and reduction," adding that "Goethe's *Fairytale* is an opera told in words."

Exaltation of man above himself—the underscoring of this

passage was the work of Novalis himself. He must have considered these words the main idea of his whole aphorism. To Novalis this exaltation of man above himself was the purpose of all purposes, the ultimate goal, the archetypal mission of poetry, and Goethe's *Fairytale*, in the form of an "opera told in words," a dramatic incident, served this purpose by means of "a process of transmutation, purification, and reduction." Novalis could scarcely have been content with those brief remarks, feeling so very strongly the wealth of ideas and images that lay hidden in Goethe's *Fairytale*.

The second effort at interpretation is found in Novalis' cycle of poems entitled *Flowers*, probably written immediately after the first visit to Goethe at Weimar. The fifth poem, entitled *The Time Has Come* reads:
"Splendid now stands the bridge, the mighty shadow recalling
    Time but alone; there rests ever the temple here now.
Images graven in stone and metal with marks of brute violence—
    Toppled are they and we see there but a loving pair.
None but envision locked in embrace the ancient dynasts,
    Know the helmsman well, know, too, the time of bliss."

The words of the title of these distichs *The Time Has Come* derive from Goethe's tale itself. They are spoken in the subterranean temple. The time of bliss which is at hand is the idea of the return of the Golden Age, the Paradise Regained—thoughts which Novalis shared with Friedrich Schlegel and which he found again in Goethe's images of his tale.

Among the fragments Novalis collected under the headline *Poetic Physiology* appears his third attempt to interpret Goethe's tale. "Our lips oft resemble the two will-o'-the-wisps in the fairytale. The eyes are loftier twins to the lips—they open and close a grotto more sacred than the mouth. The ears are the serpent greedily devouring what the will-o'-the-wisps have let fall. Mouth and eyes are similar in shape. The lashes are the lips, the apple the tongue and the palate, the iris the throat. The nose is the brow to the mouth, and the brow, nose to the eyes. Each eye has a chin in its cheekbone."

These ideas stemmed from Goethe's theory of metamorphosis, his morphological thoughts about polarity and enhancement, and they are the ones Novalis made use of in his interpretation of the *Fairytale*. Mouth and eyes are the two polarities in the human visage. But within these polarities there is an enhancement of powers. Novalis compared the upper and lower lip with the two will-o'-the-wisps in Goethe's *Fairytale,* and the eyes appear as a loftier set of twins to them. The eyes are a "more sacred grotto" than the mouth. The lips of the mouth correspond to the near bank of the river on which the green serpent lives. The eyes, symbolizing the youth and Lily, living on the far bank where they celebrate their mystic marriage, form the other polarity.

His final interpretation is found in the collection of fragments Novalis called *The General Brouillon,* probably written late in 1798 or during the early months of the following year: "Perfection speaks not merely on its own. It expresses a whole world related to itself. That is why perfection of every kind is shrouded by the veil of the Eternal Virgin which the slightest touch dissolves into magic vapor, becoming the seer's cloud chariot. She is heaven—the telescope and at once the fixed star—and therefore the manifestation of a higher world. . . . With every feature of perfection a work leaps further away from its master, into more than space and distance. With the final stroke the master sees his ostensible creation separated from himself by a chasm of thought, the span of which he himself scarcely comprehends, and across which only imagination, like the shadow of the giant yclept intelligence, can leap. At the very moment when it is to enter into full being, it becomes more than he, its creator, while he in turn becomes the organ and chattel of a higher power. The artist belongs to the work and not the work to the artist."

These thoughts about the veil of the Eternal Virgin refer directly to Goethe's *Fairytale.* The Beautiful Lily, central figure in the fantasy, is the Eternal Feminine, heaven, telescope and star. In other words, she is the source, means and object of our knowledge in the form of a "true revelation of a higher world." Novalis points to Fair Lily as the ideal human within mankind. This ideal lives in the realm of images, weaving the veil that becomes the "seer's cloud chariot." Ideas are the mediators (telescope) in the process of conception. Concepts become the objects of ultimate knowledge, like fixed stars. The realm of absolute perfection—Lily—is separated by a chasm of thought. In the *Fairytale* this chasm takes the form of the river, separating the youth from the realm of Lily. We may surmount this separation only by means of the bridge which the green serpent forms at noon, or by the shadow of the giant at night and in the morning. The serpent bridge is imagination, the shadow of the giant abstract intelligence.

On the subject of this "giant yclept intelligence" we have

another fragment from the pen of Novalis, representing a valuable supplement. "On seeing a giant it is best first to establish the position of the sun and take care that it is not the shadow of a pygmy. (About the immense effects of the little—can they not all be explained like the giant shadow of the pygmy?)" What Novalis meant to express here is that true thought carries in its innermost substance the power of a giant, but that the giant is not necessarily identical with the shadow he casts. True wisdom (the giant) is sharply distinct from its pale shadow (sophistry, sciolism). Such pygmy wisdom is incapable of achieving the knowledge of a higher world which Novalis symbolized with the veil of the Eternal Virgin.

The creation of the *Tale* remained a deep problem to Goethe himself. When Prince August of Gotha tried to read it as the revelation of a St. John reborn and asked Goethe for his own interpretation, the poet replied that he would send such an explanation, "but I do not propose to publish it until I see nine and ninety predecessors before me." Far advanced in age, in the year 1830, Goethe wrote to Carlyle, who interpreted the *Fairytale* and translated it into English, that the work was a feast of the poetic imagination that would scarcely have succeeded a second time.

The first of these "ninety nine" interpreters was Novalis. The fourfold path which he walked in his explanation prepared him for his own poetic workshop. "The true fairytale must be at once a prophetic presentation, an idealized presentation, an absolutely necessary presentation. The true storyteller is a seer into the future." To him the fairytale was "the canon of poetry." The study of Goethe's tale became the starting point for his magic idealism.

3. MAGIC IDEALISM

Novalis never regarded himself as a philosopher and he proposed no systematic structure of ideas. His own philosophical attitude he characterized as being in contrast to the empiricists of the Enlightenment such as Voltaire and to the dogmatists—"Thence the road leads to Kant, thence to Fichte, and at last to magic idealism." This magic idealism is inextricably linked with his element of poetic imagination.

He called this magic idealism an "omnipotent organ in philosophy." In other words, it was for him rather an inner faculty than an abstract doctrine. He identified it also with the "act of romanticizing." His fundamental formulation reads: "The world must be romanticized. In this way one rediscovers its original meaning. Romanticizing is nothing but a qualitative raising to a higher power. In this operation the lower self becomes identified with a higher self. Just as we ourselves are such a qualitative exponential series. This operation is still wholly unknown." Novalis used the verb "to romanticize" to characterize an act of the imagination. He never used the abstract terms "romanticism" or "The Romantic School." They are nowhere to be found in his writings. To romanticize is a function rather than a state of the soul. It cannot be defined by means of a single concept. It can only be described in terms of comparable images. Romanticizing is a "qualitative raising to a higher power," which is the very thing Novalis, in the sense of Fichte, marked as the highest mission of self-development to become "the ego of one's own ego."

Novalis availed himself of a mathematical image because he sought to convey a precise and detached picture of this complex process. His formulation was also related to the mathematical and philosophical studies he had pursued, especially his study of Kant. He posed the basic question of his magic idealism: "Is there extrasensory knowledge?" "According to Kant, pure mathematics and pure science refer to the forms of outward sensibility. What science, then, refers to the forms of inward sensibility? Is there extrasensory knowledge? Is there still another way open for going beyond oneself, reaching other beings, or being affected by them?"

The answer to this question is given in the fragmentary thoughts of his "magic idealism." They appear as a world of fragments, but they are not a fragment of a world by virtue of the centripetal power of his coherent philosophy.

The basic pattern underlying the collection of fragments that has come down to us under the title of *The General Brouillon* (its 1153 fragmentary paragraphs and aphorisms constitute almost half the known writings of Novalis in this vein) is an "attempt at a universal approach to Biblicism, the introduction to a true encyclopedism."

Novalis thought of the prototype of his "Bible" as a universal encyclopedia in the conception of the fairytale as revealed to him in Goethe's fantasy. It was in Goethe's tale, that he found "grand history symbolically rejuvenated" . . . . "The Bible begins gloriously with Paradise, the symbol of youth, and ends with the eternal kingdom, the holy city . . . the history of every man ought to be a Bible . . . a Bible is the highest mission of creative writing."

He uses the word Bible figuratively. He calls his "Bible" scientific because he thinks of it as a synthesis of knowledge, art and religion. It comprises past, present, and future. In its turn toward the future it is apocalyptic. Wholly unorthodox, he asks: "Cannot the preparation of several gospels be envisioned? Must it always be historical? . . . Is there not a Gospel of the future?"

Sermons in the spirit of Zinzendorf, works like those of Jacob Boehme, poems in the manner of Gottfried Arnold, treatises like Lessing's *Education of the Human Race,* the historical philosophy of Herder, the aesthetical education of man as given by Schiller—all these works impressed themselves on his mind and combined with his own cultural heritage. Yet the idea of his scientific bible sprang from his own spiritual experiences. As a new "encyclopedia" it was to turn in equal measure against the rationalism of the French Enlightenment and against the religious orthodoxy.

Nothing can characterize Novalis' inner attitude toward religion in more personal fashion than this passage from a letter to Just: "How your heart swells when you pick up the Bible, to find in it a token of God and immortality! How happy you must seem to yourself when you become convinced that in it you possess supernatural scripture, lasting revelation, that you can cling to its pages as though to a guiding hand into a higher sphere! Your theology is the theology of historic-critical reason, which seeks a firm foundation, inexorable proof, and finds it in a collection of documents. . . . If I am rooted less in documentary certainty, less in the letter, less in the truth and circumstance of history; if I am more inclined to track down higher influences within me and to blaze a trail of my own into the primal world . . . . you will surely not, in the makings of this religious approach, deny the prominent element of my existence—imagination."

The trail to his own "primal world"—it is the road that leads to the ideal conception of poet and priest. The "Bible"-fragments were attempts of the priestly bard to write a fable, a tale of the coming synthesis of science, art, and religion. His "Bible-art", as he called it often, flowed directly into his "Lore of Man."

Here in his psychological concepts the philosophy of Fichte became the most formative element, as Goethe's view on nature and art determined his creative work. The collection of his more than 2,000 fragments—the greater part dating from the two years immediately following the death of Sophia, appears haphazard, disjointed, without system. Yet they are always focused on the nature of man. At their core lies the philosophy of the consciousness of self. His understanding of human nature, the "lore of man," was something altogether original. There are thoughts on life and death, sleep and dream, body and spirit, day and night, flashing up in formulations that are unique. Seen by themselves, they can sometimes be irritating, but related to one another and viewed as a whole they reveal the kind of higher logic that characterizes true mysticism. Behind many of these fragments more lies hidden than mere intellectual acrobatics.

The lore of man is not only psychology but also physiology. We find, for example, the strangest notes on sleeping and waking. Novalis proceeded by the Goethean method, which saw all organic processes governed by the law of polarity and gradation. Systole and diastole, inhalation and exhalation, contraction and expansion—to him these were living forces of human nature. "Sleep is digestion of the soul. The body digests the soul. Wakefulness is the state during which the body relishes the soul. In sleep the bonds of the system are loose, in waking they are taut." Or another example: "When spirit dies it becomes man. When man dies he becomes spirit"—this sentence accepts the pre-existence and post-existence of the soul in the Platonic sense, yet in this formulation it states something quite original, especially since it is supported by the following words: "May there not be death up yonder as well, its fruit earthly birth?" pointing to the idea of metempsychosis that was to play so important a role in his *Heinrich von Ofterdingen*.

One senses that many of these thoughts are no mere toying with abstract antitheses, but that Novalis has learned something of the deeper layers of human nature by listening to the more secret and intimate rhythms of the heart. Perhaps this is the reason for the magic spell which the *Fragments* have continued to cast over readers ever since their first appearance in the *Athenaeum*.

They are "literary seedlings" which Novalis scattered day by day and nursed like a gardener. It must not be forgotten that these thousands of notes represent an hour-by-hour account of his efforts at contemplation, the true diary of a mystic who watched over his own soul in constant vigilance and self-discipline, and who therefore was entitled to write: "The world of the spirit has indeed opened up to us even now. It is always manifest. Were we suddenly to become as resilient as we should be, we would recognize that we live in the midst of that world."

4. THE NOVICES OF SAIS

"One reached the goal at Sais; he lifted the veil of the goddess,
Only to see, forsooth, wonder of wonders—himself."

This distich, written as early as the spring of 1798, anticipated the story of *Hyacinth and Rosebud,* which formed the core of the discourses of the *Novices of Sais.*

The little tale itself begins with a description of the lad Hyacinth. He dwelt "far toward the evening" but his wandering led him to the north, the south, and the east, ending at the "abode of the everlasting seasons," in other words, a supernatural region beyond space and time.

At the outset of the story, Hyacinth and Rosebud love each other with the innocent fondness of children. The flowers and beasts know of their friendship, and the lizzard sings that Rosebud has grown so blind from her love, that on one occasion she took her own mother for Hyacinth.

This state of innocent childhood draws to an end when an old man comes and for three days tells Hyacinth of faraway countries. Before he departs he leaves a book "no man can read." Because of this book, Hyacinth "begins a new course of life" and is as though "reborn." The rebirth is achieved by a "strange old woman in the woods" who casts the book into the fire. From her he learns that he must himself go out to seek the "mother of all things, the veiled Virgin." Hyacinth sets out on the road to the abode of the "everlasting seasons." The flowers about the crystal spring show him the way, until he falls asleep where "dream alone may lead into the Holy of Holies." Amid the sound of supernatural music "all seemed familiar to him, albeit in a splendor never seen before." When at last he lifts the veil of the heavenly Virgin, Rosebud sinks into his arms.

Hidden behind this simple tale is the basic theme of Novalis' whole world outlook: the highest mission of self-development is to become "the ego's ego." Hyacinth and Rosebud are torn asunder only to be at last reunited on a higher level. A new course of life began with the meeting of the old man; but the mysterious book no one could read had to be burned by the old woman so that

Hyacinth could be reborn. Only through the burning of the book did he learn how he could become whole.

In interpreting such stories we gain little insight by asking merely the meaning of this symbol or that. The tale of Hyacinth and Rosebud tells us of a process of transmutation, of seeking and finding, of a higher reunion. This higher union between Hyacinth and Rosebud must be developed through several stages. Both have been united since their birth. But this unity must now be won in conscious struggle. So Hyacinth and Rosebud are separated. Only separation can make possible reunion at a higher level.

We can distinguish three main stages that lead to this reunion. The old man, who for three days tells Hyacinth about faraway lands and in the end gives a book no one can read, causes him to embark upon a new course of life. But he feels "reborn" only when the old woman burns the book and tells him how he may become healthy. The first step in this rebirth came from the old man, the second from the old woman. The third step he must take himself. He falls asleep, for only a dream can lead him into the Holy of Holies.

This Holy of Holies is the higher, divine Self. It seems to rest in a temple that can be reached only by passing through three antechambers. The man who leaves the book no one can read tells of faraway lands, in other words of supernatural regions. This is the subject of the book he leaves. But what is written in the book in mere letters must first be transmuted within the soul. That is why the old woman burns the book. This burning of mere book-learning purifies the soul in preparation for spiritual vision. The soul can now become "healthy".

In the end Hyacinth attains something neither the old man nor the woman could give him. Within Hyacinth rests the power of true child-nature. It is this childlike element that enables him to reach the abode of the everlasting seasons, a world in which space and time are canceled. The last incident is the lifting of the veil of the Eternal Virgin, the reunion with Rosebud. The rediscovery of Rosebud is the last degree of self-revelation, the "wonder of wonders."

This story, undoubtedly first written separately, was later taken into his *Novices of Sais*. The two works supplement each other. The element of inner unity which they share may be described as the "sacred road to physical science." A fragmentary sentence, recurring almost verbatim in letters written in January

1799, tells us: "This divine spark of an understanding nature dwelt even in Spinoza. Plotinus, perhaps moved by Plato, was the first to enter this sanctuary in the true spirit, and no one since has penetrated it so deeply. . . . Goethe is to become the liturgist of this physical science—he understands the temple service perfectly."

Surely Novalis' studies concerning Plato, Plotinus, and Goethe must have had a share in the ideas of the *Novices,* a share equal to, if not greater than that of his Freiberg teacher, Werner. Heretofore the figure of the preceptor of the *Novices* has been taken exclusively to represent a portrait of Werner. It has been overlooked that to Novalis it was Goethe who was "the liturgist of the new physical science."

Goethe in his Apollonian contemplation of nature had sought to revive the spirit of Greece. His Faust witnessed the miracle of the Classical Walpurgis Night and united himself with Helen of Troy. But Novalis, in his Dionysiac-Hermetic thirst for self-knowledge, turned his eyes to the mysteries of Egypt and was led into the temple of Isis.

The cult of Isis, attaining importance only in the late Egyptian period, still later coalesced with the Hellenic mysteries of Demeter. Demeter-Ceres was the *dea natura,* Mother Earth. Like Isis with the Horus child, Demeter with Jacchus (the Dionysus child) was a familiar image of the ancient rites, a pre-Christian image that found its way into the transformed Christian cult of the Madonna.

Novalis made Sais his scene rather than the ancient centers of the Isis-cult at Memphis or Abydos; he was, most probably, influenced by Plato's *Timaeus* and *Critias,* where the priestly sages initiated Solon into the secrets of the dawn of history. Actually the *Novices* express neither the Egyptian nor the Platonic heritage. Rather do these discourses constitute a true prologue to the natural philosophy of Romanticism. The novices were "drawn to Sais by the call of antiquity," they hoped to find enlightenment from the "custodians of the temple archives." But their preceptor is also to be the vehicle for "new gospels," "true inspirations." Beyond doubt, his features resemble those of Goethe, the "liturgist of the new physical science who best knows the temple service." But his image is timeless. He is *the* teacher.

The basic theme of the *Novices of Sais* is the understanding of nature in its deeper creative powers, the encompassing of the

Book of Nature as a new "Bible." This book is a cipher script no man can read at first. But what happened to Hyacinth in the story also happened to the novices in the fragmentary novel. The language of nature is revealed through the teacher.

The Preceptor speaks only at the beginning and the end. His words form, as it were, the alpha and omega of the new natural philosophy.

The intrinsic thought envisioned by Novalis was that the true scientist is at once the herald of a new gospel. The true scientist is at the same time the real artist. Only he may set foot in the temple of nature. Here too it is Goethe who may have furnished the immediate model: "The inward life of a poet, trained senses, a plain and God-fearing mind—these are the essential prerequisites of a true friend of nature." Nature at first appears to us as no more than a "fearful mill of death," the interplay of endless fission and atomization. Only by an act of free will can man redeem himself from this "dreadful prison." The power of nature would only slowly destroy our organs of thought and drive us to insanity. Man must make himself master over the disintegrating powers of nature. His moral freedom tames nature.

Moral freedom is the talisman by which man becomes aware of his higher nature. "Vigilant man feels himself master of the world. His self hovers mightily above the abyss. . . . The meaning of the world is reason. The world exists for the sake of reason." In the course of developing freedom, reason is capable of ever higher stages, "until some day it becomes the divine image of its own work, the scene of a true church." The moral sense opens the heart of nature, vanquishing her destructive trends.

The true novice of nature must transcend the analytical power of reason, which encompasses merely the destructive processes of nature. He must train himself in thought, to the end that he shall be able to use "reason in comprehending nature." We must not merely think; we must feel as well. "Thought is but a dream of sensation, a feeling that has died, a life that has grown pale, grey, and feeble." Novalis mentions how the practice of "undivided attention" may give rise to new thoughts "or a new kind of perception."

Just as the thoughts about nature which the novices voice seem to relate to Goethe's scientific approach, so does the doctrine of moral freedom in the book as a whole appear related to the philosophy of Schiller. Novalis submitted that only by the fusion of thought with feeling, by the concentrating on sense impressions within the self, does man experience true freedom. He called this experience "interplay" in obvious connection with Schiller's idea of the impulsion of play (Spieltrieb) as harmonizing the sensuous and the reasoning impulses, (see Schiller, *Letters on the Aesthetical Education of Man*, Letter XIV) ; for Novalis said of this "interplay": "It is very curious that only in this interplay does man grow truly aware of his peculiarity, his specific freedom, and that, when he does, it seems to him as though he were awakening from a deep sleep, as though only now he were at home in the world."

After the first three novices have spoken, Novalis allows a "fair youth" to say: "The poets alone have sensed what the nature of man could be." This passage, in which Novalis lets the fair youth speak of the nature of water and fire, is superbly beautiful. In the interplay between fire and water lies nature's secret of love and "even sleep is no more than the floodtide of that invisible world ocean, while awakening is the coming of its ebbtide." The fair youth then concludes with the fantasy images of Hyacinth, as though he himself were the loving lad, feeling himself "within Nature as though in the bosom of his chaste bride."

Scarcely are these words of the fair youth spoken, which reach the height of a dialogue of the type found in Plato's *Symposium*, when the climax and the end of the discourses come. The Preceptor draws close again and has brought a shining precious ruby. Here Novalis, following in the footsteps of Plato, describes how the sages at Sais preserved the last traces "of that lost ancient race" of Atlantis, the relics of a tradition under which it could be said that "the life of the universe is an everlasting, thousand-voiced discourse."

When we hear the voice of the Preceptor again at the end of the fragmentary book, we needs must recall the words that Novalis wrote in the first person at the end of the first part of this novel, which is called "The Novice" in contrast to the second part, "Nature." "The Preceptor I cannot and will not understand. Yet do I love him, incomprehensible though he be, I know he understands me. Never has he spoken counter to my feelings and my desires. . . ." and he ends with words that relate to the veiled image of Isis at Sais: "If, by yon inscription, none who is mortal can lift the veil, then must we seek to become immortal. Whoever refuses to lift it is no true novice of Sais."

The lifting of the veil, significantly foretold in the Hyacinth-Rosebud tale, becomes a symbol of the quest for self-knowledge. Thus the tale is the germ cell of the book. It is itself a fully finished whole, while the *Novices* remained but a fragment of a much larger project. From the viewpoint of language, the *Novices* shows greater maturity. The fairytale within the novel contains many commonplace images: "Pretty as a picture," "she looked as though she had been painted," "her proportions were like those of a little doll," "charming sounds." In the *Novices* there are scarcely any trite adjectives. The language throughout has a lofty aspect, even though long passages of reflection on natural philosophy are interspersed in the conversation among the novices, slowing up the flow of the story.

"The great strength of *Die Lehrlinge zu Sais* lies in its combination of romantic emotion with a naturalist's love of nature. The interpretations of nature made by the Novices are like a set of variations on the theme of the relation of Man to Nature" writes Stephen Spender in his preface to the newly translated edition of the *Novices of Sais* (with sixty drawings by Paul Klee; published by Curt Valentin, New York 1949) and he continues: "Each Novice who expounds his philosophy, organizes a vision of Nature around his idea, with a power like that of a snow crystal forming out of a drop of vapor..... This is a curiously interior world; a world of pure art and pure contemplation, of imagist poems, and an intense, glowing, yet humorous and meticulous imagination."

In the midst of his Freiberg studies, Novalis wrote these dialogues as his first poetic myth which grew on its own beyond his fragmentary collections of aphorisms, jotted down in diary form. To be sure, the little work remained a fragment, resembling the fluctuating style of his hundredfold fleeting thoughts. The influences that led to this first attempt at a novel came from several sides: studies under Werner at the Freiberg mining academy; the world of Goethe's natural science, Schiller's philosophy of freedom; the visit to the Dresden art gallery, especially the impact of Raphael's Sistine Madonna. The very title of the novel *Die Lehrlinge zu Sais* suggests that Novalis sought to create a work that might take its place by the side of Goethe's *Wilhelm Meisters Lehrjahre*. At any rate, the similarity between the two metaphoric words, the apprenticeship of Meister and the apprentices at Sais, is no mere chance. Novalis voiced on the occasion of his *Faith and Love* the demand for a book in the form of *Natalie's Apprenticeship,* in obvious competition with Goethe's novel.

However diversely suggestions and images from without may have affected him, the innermost core of this first work lay in Novalis' unique experience with Sophie. Remaining a fragment, it combines the charm of poetic spontaneity with the obvious shortcomings of the earliest attempts of a novelwriter.

5. THE TALE OF EROS AND FABLE

The tale of Eros and Fable is told by Klingsor, the minstrel, at the end of the first part of *Heinrich von Ofterdingen.* It was written long before the novel, however, a fully rounded and independent creation. Often it is simply referred to as *the* Tale of Novalis, leading us into the innermost workshop of his poetry. Klingsor, the narrator of this story, bears the features of Goethe, whose fairytale, which concluded his *Tales of the German Refugees,* inspired the fantasy of Novalis and influenced some passages even stylistically.

Goethe once confessed that his tale challenged interpretation "since it intertwines images, ideas, and concepts." This observation applies to Novalis' story as well. Concepts are expressed in allegory. Allegory personifies the concept. Here alone is it proper to inquire into intellectual meaning. Ideas are encompassed by symbols. They are the expression of a process, a function. Images, finally, are the real element of a tale as such. They are myths of free imagination. We must focus on their metamorphosis, asking what it is that becomes disenchanted, deciphered, redeemed—or, in the language of Novalis, "unveiled."

The difficulty in answering this question lies in the fact that a work like Novalis' tale is made up of all three elements, intertwined in shifting sequences. The characters that appear in the tale bear names from the most diverse elements of Greek mythology (Eros, the Parcae, Perseus, the Sphinx), from Nordic-Germanic legend (Freya), from Arabian sources (Ginnistan), from astronomy (Arcturus, Moon)—or they are given general names like Fable, Mother, Father, Scribe, and lastly, in wholly individual fashion, Sophia.

Three main themes, mentioned by the poet himself in his fragmentary notes, are freely interwoven. The tale is an allegorical myth of nature, it is a symbolic drama of original sin and redemption; it is finally an imaginative apotheosis of Sophia.

At first glance the wealth of images and the shifting scenes and themes are confusing. We miss the simplicity of structure we encountered in the tale of Hyacinth. Yet this maze and network of symbols and allegories has an inward order, once we recognize that the tale plays in four different worlds. Dante's *Divina Commedia* proceeded from Earth by way of the Inferno and Purgatory to Paradiso, and we glimpse these four worlds in Novalis' tale as well.

In the story the world of man on earth is called "at home." Here, at the outset, stand the cradles of Eros and Fable. The Underworld, into which Fable descends thrice, is the tale's "Inferno." The Realm of the Moon is the abode of temptation. The Realm of King Arcturus, to the North, where sleeps the Princess Freya, awaiting her awakener, is the spiritual world, the Paradiso, the home of Sophia, who after a period of separation is reunited with her consort Arcturus.

It is noteworthy that thirteen main characters appear in the tale (Eros, Fable, Ginnistan, Father, Mother, the Scribe, the Old Hero, Perseus, the Sphinx, the Moon, Freya, Arcturus, and finally Sophia) and that the scene shifts thirteen times among the four worlds. When one endeavors to represent these baffling changes of scene in graphic fashion, the structure shows an astonishing harmony. It is the architecture of a fully rounded drama, with rising and falling action. Indeed, on passing the middle, at the eighth stage, one finds that the whole plot begins to unravel.

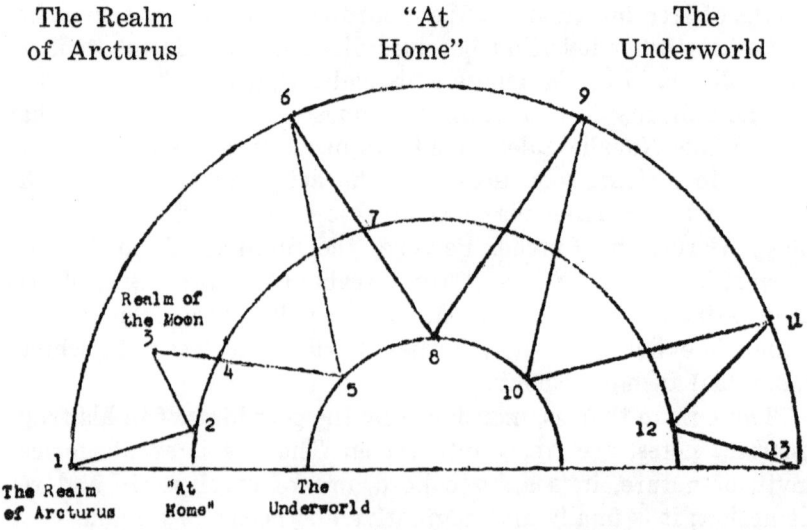

Before looking at the individual scenes, let us sum up the basic theme of all these "images, ideas, and concepts": Sophia, doomed to separation from her divine spouse, seeks ultimately to be reunited with Arcturus forever. To bring about the return of the Golden Age, Eros must be redeemed from the Realm of the Moon to awaken Freya, daughter of the gods; Fable must vanquish the Scribe, the Underworld, and the Parcae, before she can sing her paean of praise to heavenly Sophia. Thus the tale tells how Eros became the power of pure love and Fable develops the force of divine poetry, in order that Sophia, reunited with Arcturus, may become the everlasting priestess of the heart.

"The long night had just begun," the tale starts out, in the Realm of Arcturus. It is the age of iron and darkness, in which war and error rule, rather than peace and wisdom. King Arcturus and his daughter Freya play with screeds "on which were inscribed sacred symbols made up of heavenly constellations." Arcturus holds sway to the north of the world. (In astronomy, Arcturus is a star in the constellation Boeotes, near the Big Dipper and the Pole Star. North is the region of midnight, traditionally looked upon by mystics as the realm of pure spirituality.) Here, it has become "night," hidden from the eyes of man. But the King exclaims prophetically: "Iron, hurl thou thy sword into the world, that they learn where dwells peace." Peace is Freya, the Princess, awaiting her awakener. From her womb the world shall be kindled anew. Night shall fade, the ice melt, the Iron Age give way to the Golden Age.

But for this to happen, Eros and Fable must travel their paths, to suffer inner change and purification. This the story images tell us in the symbolic language of sin and redemption.

"At home," on earth, Eros lies in his cradle, together with his foster-sister Fable, under the care of the suckling-nurse Ginnistan who represents the imagination. In contrast to Ginnistan stands the Scribe, whom Novalis characterized as "petrifying and petrified intellect."

Sophia, the "woman like unto a goddess" dips the sheets on which the Scribe has written into a vessel standing on an altar. She returns to the Scribe only those on which the writing has endured. The others are washed clean in the water. Sometimes Sophia sprinkles Fable and Eros with the holy water from the altar vessel, and in the blue haze a thousand images are revealed. But whenever a droplet touches the Scribe, it turns into numbers and geometric figures which he strings around his neck.

The Father brings a magnetic needle, and the Scribe notes down his remarks, but the sheet, dipped into the water by Sophia, turns white. The words set down by the "petrified intellect" do not withstand the insight of a higher wisdom about magnetism. Ginnistan, with her power of creative imagination, then breathes upon the magnetic needle which is transformed into a serpent biting its own tail—an age-old symbol of mystical insight and self-knowledge.

Eros himself grows as he holds the magnetic needle: he gains in self-knowledge. Fable, embraced by Eros, writes something on the sheets which stands the test. Eros, in company of Ginnistan, plans to travel to Arcturus, to awaken Freya, a journey which the Scribe seeks to prevent in vain.

We follow Eros on his way with Ginnistan. But Ginnistan continues to be the chaotic power of imagination and is therefore held fast in the Realm of the Moon. Indeed, the Moon himself is her father. Father Moon gives Eros and Ginnistan the key to his treasure house. What they see there is like a glimpse into a Dantesque Inferno, a descent into the dawn world and the realm of the dead. Finally, despite all the turmoil of shipwreck and battle, of flood and flame, they see an arch that rests above the flood; on it sits Sophia, the altar vessel in her hand, by the side of a man wreathed in oak leaves—a vision of the future reunion with Arcturus. On the waters floats a flower. Fable sits on a lily pad, holding a harp in her hands. The chalice of the lily enfolds Eros and a girl, like a single blossom—a vision of bliss to come.

Eros, however, forgetting the store of holy water Sophia gave him on his journey, sinks into the arms of his suckling-nurse in abandoned slumber. The journey to Arcturus is broken, the liberation of Freya postponed.

While Eros succumbs to the temptations of the Realm of the Moon, Fable, on her part, escapes perils, unleashed by the plotting of the Scribe, who forces the Mother to slavery, imprisons the Father, and demolishes the altar of Sophia. Fable descends to the Underworld and faces the questioning Sphinx. The discourse between Fable and the Sphinx recalls Goethe's *Tale* even in the language structure. Fable learns from the Sphinx, that love is "in the realm of fancy." Asked where Sophia is, the Sphinx gives no answer, for Fable must provide it herself: "Sophia and love"—that is the mystery Fable must herself solve. Before that solution can be achieved, Fable comes upon the Parcae. Fable, helping them to spin the fate, sings a song. It comes at the turning point of the whole tale.

Fable proclaims that she can spin the fateful threads of all men into a single thread, for all are to merge into one higher life. But scarcely has Fable's song died away, when the Scribe himself appears in the Underworld, announcing to Fable that her Mother must suffer death in the flames on the morrow. Fable fearlessly mocks the Scribe, escapes him once again, and reaches the Realm of Arcturus. Fable brings glad tidings from the Underworld: "Soon shall wisdom return and the heart be transfigured."

The Crown of the North circles the head of Arcturus. In his left hand the King holds the Lily, in his right a scale. Fable returns to earth with the lyre which Arcturus has given her. There she encounters her worn and sorrowing Mother, soon to be burned on the pyre reared by the Scribe.

Ginnistan and Eros have also returned to earth, coming from the moon, but Eros falls asleep on the bosom of Ginnistan. The sun falls in the sea, a burned-out cinder, but "the flame had grown splendid beyond expression. . . the flame grew whiter and more powerful as the sun turned paler," it flared up toward the realm of Arcturus. In vain the Scribe seeks to quench it.

The death of the Mother, the fall of the sun, the coming of the flame - these are the turning-points in the tale. Again escaping the pursuit of the Scribe, Fable descends once more into the Underworld, where she confesses before the Sphinx that love is the everlasting mystery of the world, abiding with Sophia. At these words the Sphinx writhes wretchedly.

Fable again gains the presence of Arcturus, and to her question "Has the flame arrived?" he replies: "It has come. The night is over. The ice is melting."

Fable, descending to the Underworld for the last time, destroys the power of the Parcae and then, with the aid of Arcturus, gathers the ashes of the Mother. The house has crumbled into ruins, but from them new life burgeons. Sophia stands at the rebuilt altar. Eros in armor is at her feet. The Father is asleep, Ginnistan hovering over him. Sophia greets Fable as "the soul of our life...Yours is the Phoenix....wake now the bridegroom." Sophia then seizes the Mother's urn and empties the ashes into the altar vessel, from which she bids all drink. The Mother's spirit permeates all and Sophia pronounces: "The great mystery is manifest to all: Within each dwells the heavenly Mother to bear each child forevermore. Feel ye not the sweet birth in the beating of your breast?"

The world is again in a state of eternal spring. Iron, the Hero, gives the sword to Eros, that he may awaken Freya. Perseus presents Fable with a distaff on which she is to spin an unbreakable thread of gold - a new destiny. From the dome Arcturus descends with Sophia and they solemnize the consecration of the new couple. The final tableau of the tale gathers together all the characters, with the exception of the Scribe, who is not even mentioned again, when Sophia proclaims: "The Mother is among us." Fable consecrates the new realm, for the struggle has ended in love (Eros) and peace (Freya) - now united for good -, and at the last she chants a paean of praise to Sophia, the "eternal priestess of the heart."

The Tale is a revelation of Novalis' self. The foundation stone underlying the idea of the work seems to have been laid as early as the time of lamentation over the death of Sophia. Ten days after her death Novalis wrote to Just: "...Born soft, my reason has expanded steadily, subtly displacing my heart from its possessions. Sophia restored the lost throne to my heart. Perhaps her death may return the reins to the usurper!—who then would surely root out the heart. Even now I have been very sensitive to his cold indifference. Perhaps I shall yet be saved by the invisible world and its power, a power that has slumbered within me heretofore. Day by day the idea of God grows more welcome to me."

Sophia von Kühn restored the heart to its lost throne. The usurper who sought to root out the heart with cold indifference - is the "Scribe" within Novalis. As Faust saw his lower nature reflected in Mephistopheles, so Novalis saw himself in the figure of the Scribe. The heart is the true mother of Eros. The Scribe can destroy but the heart of the body, not that of the soul. In the Greek myth the mother of Eros is Chaos. Here in the tale she must be burned, that she may be "in our midst" as the new order, as Sophia says repeatedly. The Scribe cannot destroy this spiritual element of the Mother. It is insolubly bound up with the theme of the "flame."

What is this flame? It is kindled from the pyre. "The sun stood in the sky...the mighty flame drew in its borrowed light... the flame grew whiter and more powerful as the sun grew

paler...the flame had grown splendid beyond expression...
slowly it rose upward and drifted away toward the North (into
the Realm of Arcturus). When the Scribe had tried in vain to
quench the flame, Arcturus solemnly proclaimed: "It (the
flame) has come. The night is over. The ice is melting. My consort (Sophia) shows herself from afar." The Mother, in turn, he
calls his enemy who has now been destroyed - Chaos, the mother
of Eros, the concept at the bottom of sensual animal love. So long
as it is not transmuted, it is the enemy of Arcturus, who with
his consort Sophia is the representative of spiritual love.

The flame therefore stands in curious contrast to the Mother
who is burned. It looms above all the characters of the tale, for
by its agency all is transmuted. The ice melts; the Parcae die,
the fate they had been spinning becomes a new destiny; Eros is
purged and purified: Ginnistan is rejuvenated and rendered immortal; Sophia, finally, may return to Arcturus forever. The
flame alone can withstand the Scribe. It is not subject to his
curse. It is the secret of the world which Sophia and her own
must preserve. The flame is mightier than all the characters
in the tale, and it is the principle by which the Golden Age may
come back.

The flame is the symbol of Christ, the heart of the world
which the "usurper seeks in vain to root out." "The heart is the
key to the world," Novalis wrote in a fragmentary note, a direct
commentary on the theme, for he added: "In the same way that
Christ is the key to the world"; and soon afterward: "Ordinary
life is a priestly service, almost like that of the vestals. We are
busied with nothing but the maintenance of a sacred and mysterious flame." And later to Friedrich Schlegel: "The antipathy
of light and shadow, the yearning for the clear, hot, penetrating ether, the *unknown sanctity*, the Vesta in Sophia, the mixture of the romantic elements of all ages, petrifying and petrified
intellect, Arcturus...the spirit of life, single features as mere
arabesques - it is in this light that my tale should be seen."

It is because the flame is the symbol of the Christ spirit
that drinking from the vessel holding the ashes of the Mother
becomes "divine," a communion ceremony, of which Sophia
proclaims: "The great mystery is manifest to all and remains
unfathomable forever. In agony shall the new world be born and
in tears shall the ashes be dissolved in the drink of life everlasting."

Related to the image of the flame is that of the Phoenix; for it is the Phoenix which rises from its own ashes. This is an ancient alchemist symbol for the resurrection of Christ. In alchemy the Phoenix was identical with the *Lapis,* the "stone of gold," and characterized the renewal of life. That is why at the end Sophia says to Fable: "Yours is the Phoenix." And Fable perches on the wings of the Phoenix, hovering above the throne that has finally become transformed into a marriage bed. The meaning of this transformation is what the alchemists termed the "chymical marriage." (See C. G. Jung, *Psychologie und Alchemie,* Zürich 1946).

Fable under the influence of the Scribe is but the didactic prosody of rationalism. But Fable on the pinions of the Phoenix becomes the priestess of Christ.

Novalis himself was in fact a "Scribe" on the way to conquering petrified and petrifying intellect. Ultimately he achieved the union between the poet (Fable) and the wisdom of the divine world (Sophia). To be sure, there were times when his many scattered fragments, notes, excerpts, and commentaries that filled his notebook must have seemed to him like the pages of the Scribe which Sophia dipped into the water in the altar vessel, and returned blank and expunged.

The three main powers of the world, beauty (embodied in Fable), love (Eros) and wisdom (Sophia), reunited by the sacred communion, make the final tableau possible. It is an apocalyptic vision of the future. It appears as a metamorphosis of the vision of Eros and Ginnistan in the treasure house of the Moon. There they see a flower floating on the waters. Divine figures sit on an arch spanning the stream. Uppermost is Sophia, the vessel in her hand, beside a man wreathed in oak leaves. A lily pad on which Fable sits bends over the floating flower. Within the flower is Eros embracing a girl, the two appearing as a single figure. The reference to the flower should be noted for in certain respects it anticipates what is offered in *Heinrich von Ofterdingen* as the dream of the Blue Flower. The Flower keeps the "mystery of the world," the birth of the divine within the soul. Appearing in the Realm of the Moon as a prophetic promise, it is achieved at the end of the tale by the process of purification of Eros and change of Fable. Eros receives the sword of Michael, the heavenly hero, to set Freya free. Fable gets the distaff to spin a new destiny.

But a third achievement is still essential. The Scribe, of whose end we are not told, vanishes from the scene of the story. "At a certain stage of consciousness there is no evil even now, and it is this consciousness that shall become permanent," wrote Novalis. He speaks of the annihilation of evil, designating it as the isolated and isolating principle. It is embodied in the Scribe, but his power to isolate is finally paralyzed. After all the destruction he has wrought, those who received the ashes of the Mother at the altar "feel the sweet birth beating in their breast."

Sophia is the central figure in this story of rebirth. Without her the little work would not pulse with the heart's blood of living creation. Sophia bears allegorical traits (the personification of wisdom); she appears as a symbol (the Eternal Feminine that draws us upward into the heavenly world); and she is, in addition, an altogether individual figure in the poet's fantasy - the idealized character of his bridge. The tale becomes the apotheosis of Sophia as the bride of the soul, who achieves the rebirth within the poet, becoming priestess in his heart.

Novalis wrought this first *Kunstmärchen* of Romanticist fantasy as a bridge that took him from his philosophical studies into the realm of the Muses. Not everything in this tale is poetically convincing. The influence of Goethe's tale is evident; the dialogues between Fable and Sphinx appear like copies, the initiation scene at the end of these two tales are very similar. In contrast to his later poems there is a lack of unity and simplicity. The "Arabesque-element", of which he himself wrote in connection with his tale, appears often in a confused exuberance of images and intermingled actions. This is particularly true in the scenes in the underworld with the Parcae. The mixture of Greek mythology (especially in regard to Apuleius' *Amor and Psyche*) and medieval alchemical symbols is often disturbing. It sometimes appears as a result of hastily disgested and transferred excerpts from his reading of theosophical and alchemical books during his Freiberg years.

Undoubtedly, Novalis experimented with his little tale. He himself did not seem to have considered it as a work which could stand on its own. Thus he took it into the ninth chapter of *Heinrich von Ofterdingen* and let it be told by Klingsor. Yet the content reveals a scope of apocalyptical magnitude. There are passages of beauty and a wealth of images unparalleled in the works of Romanticist fantasy. Such verses as Fable sings in view of the Phoenix anticipate the character and tone of the *Hymns to the Night* and the *Devotional Songs*. The tale, as the glorification of the heart, is a landmark on the road to Novalis' religious poetry.

6. THE HYMNS TO THE NIGHT

None of the poetic works of Novalis struck roots in his heart as early as did the *Hymns to the Night*. Their core is the immediate experience of the death of his beloved. We actually have letter passages from the time before Sophia's death that presage the state of mind from which the *Hymns* were later to take form. The process of inner growth which the *Hymns* underwent took three years. Form and content of the work clearly show that while it is deeply rooted in those months of grief, its emotional depth could not possibly have taken final form at that time.

The original impulse that led to the *Hymns* and the *Devotional Songs* lay in an experience which Novalis confided to Carolina Just in a letter one week after Sophia's death. He called the death of his beloved a betrothal in the higher sense, and then he added: "Must I not thank God that he has so soon made manifest to me my vocation to eternity? Is it not a vocation to apostolic office?"

The six hymns form a fully rounded whole, though at first glance it might seem that the individual parts are held together but superficially. They had outgrown the fragmentary character that marked so much of Novalis' work. Except for *Blossom Dust* and *Faith and Love*, it is the only work that appeared in print during the poet's lifetime.

The first hymn begins with a paean in praise of light, which like a king invests each earthly being with its divine image. In the poetic language this king is the omnipotent God the Father, resting in hidden enchantment in the world. The hymn inquires anxiously: "What if Light never returned to its children?" King is the name given to light, and like Arcturus in Klingsor's tale this king dwells in a heavenly sphere. Without his consort "Night," and the "World's Queen," he remains hidden in his realm. Night is the mother of all things, the herald of sacred worlds, like Sophia in the tale, keeper of the mystery of the world. Light is the creator of all things, but Night is maternal wisdom, whose daughter is Love.

Such are the terms in which the first hymn describes the

beginnings of all existence - space and time, day and night, the omnipotence and omniscience of the world, from which the mystery of love may be awakened within man.

This first hymn falls into three sections. In the first the poet sings the praise of light in its creative manifestations. Then he wends his way downward to the inner depths of night. Hidden under the mantle of night is the eternal Mother, the "World's Queen." She finally sends the "sun of the night," his beloved. It is she who makes night appear as the life to which he awakens.

The second hymn sings the praises of sleep. The unawakened know sleep but as a shadow. Yet to "night's consecrated ones" sleep is sacred, a herald of the gods holding the key to the world of the blissful. Life itself, unconscious of its own creative power, rests within sleep.

The third hymn, in which we find almost word for word phrases from Novalis' diary of May 13, 1797, transfigures what he felt at the grave of his beloved Sophia. The mound turns to a cloud of dust. Eons drift away into the distance. The self is reborn. The bonds of earthly birth are torn asunder. The inward vision in which he grasped the hands of his beloved, and in which his tears became an indestructible cord, is the "first dream, alone of its kind" - in other words, a "true dream", bestowed on "night's consecrated one" by "true" sleep. It is a dream which the beloved - sun of the night - turns to reality.

As the first hymn sings of the mystery of matter, hinting at the secret of the human body ("consume thou my body in the flame of spirit") ; and as the second hymn sings of sleep as the life that carries existence and joins the souls; so the third hymn is dedicated to the dream. It is in dreams that the night rises to awareness. Through them body and life attain consciousness. But just as the sleep of the second hymn is not ordinary, unconscious sleep, so the dreams that are meant are not everyday dreams, but "the first dream, the only one of its kind." It is the event in consciousness by which the poet undergoes inward rebirth, by which are "burst the bonds of birth, the fetters of Light." Let us recall an earlier sentence from the fragments dealing with the study of Fichte: "We are close to waking when we dream that we dream." It marks precisely the mood at the end of the third hymn.

The fourth hymn heralds the awakening from dream. It shows us the encounter with death. Sleep was the messenger, dream the herald of union with the higher world. But death is the creator himself who makes the union come true. The death of which Novalis speaks here is not merely something that prevails only at the hour of dying. It is a power that can turn "night" into "day" in human consciousness. Man can grasp himself in the "ego's ego." That happens not by the destructive power of the Grim Reaper but by the grace of Christ. In Christ death becomes new life.

That is why the fourth hymn begins with the image of a "pilgrimage to the Holy Sepulchre." But this pilgrimage is not the end; it is the beginning. To "night's consecrated one" death becomes a foretaste of the "crystal wave which, unseen by common sight, has its source in the dark womb of the mound at whose foot breaks the earthly tide." He stands on the "boundary" of the world, the threshold between light and night, the senses and the spirit. In death new life comes into being, for "indestructible stands the Cross."

The fourth hymn is the inward axis of the work. As the hymn of death it is also the chant of the cross. It rests on its own - it is the core, the middle. Now, toward the end, the free verse that slowly liberated itself from the rhythmic prose of the beginning passes into the purest form of rhymed lyricism. If we mark the whole fourth hymn as the central turning-point, we must understand the poem at its end as the middle of the middle.

Here it is no longer "downward wend I my way" - the descent into the depths of night, of sleep, of dream. Here the opposite path becomes actuality - "I wander across," across into the realm where the self shall lie in the bosom of love. The bosom of the world's love - Christ and Sophia," the primordial motto of Novalis' life - here it returns at the hub of his *Hymns*.

In the manuscript the poem consisted of twenty-four lines, but in the printed edition of the *Athenaeum* it appeared in twenty-eight. Just as the first three hymns up to this point had carried and sublimated the story of Sophia as their keynote, so it returns once again in the first fourteen lines of the poem. The second half of the poem, however, turns toward Christ, who henceforth becomes the keynote of all the hymns that follow.

The experience Novalis underwent at the grave of Sophia turned into the parable of the bosom of love. The prototype of that parable is Christ. The earthly token of love is the feminine element, Sophia. The cosmic prototype of love is the spiritual-masculine element - Christ.

Only in this way can we understand the difficult passage that is to be found at the precise middle of the twenty-eight-line poem, where soon after the words "I gaze from above down below upon thee," ("Ich schaue von oben herunter nach dir"), still applying to Sophia, the beloved, we suddenly read:

> O! sauge, Geliebter,
> Gewaltig mich an,
> Dass ich entschlummern
> Und lieben kann.

The expression is formulated with highly individual boldness. Here it is Christ who is the beloved (*Geliebter*), who seeks to bring him into the sphere, to drink deeply of him, to "draw him close" (*ansaugen*), as the original German puts it. The child suckles its mother's milk unconsciously. It is an unconscious, instinctive act of nature. But to be "sucked close" by the power of Christ is a superconscious act of grace. The words "O! sauge, Geliebter, gewaltig mich an" are a prayer, a humble imploration, for they go on: "Ich fühle des Todes / Verjüngende Flut, / Zu Balsam und Aether / Verwandelt mein Blut -/ Ich lebe bei Tage / Voll Glauben und Mut / Und sterbe die Nächte / In heiliger Glut."

This little poem was polished by Novalis like a precious gem. For this reason it is useful to compare the second version with the manuscript. The version for publication shows a marked maturity that may be traced through the slightest figure of speech. The pronoun "I" is thrice repeated in the first fourteen lines and thrice in the second fourteen. The first fourteen lines are followed by a dash, a clear hint calling attention to the internal caesura! Another dash, preceding the last four lines, gently points to a further stage in the metamorphosis. ("Ich lebe bei Tage / Voll Glauben und Mut / Und sterbe die Nächte / In heiliger Glut.") After the sense of rejuvenation by the power of death, as experienced in being "suckled close" by Christ, the self now leads a double life by "day" and by "night" - in other words, it continues to serve as a denizen of the earth, yet knows its true home in heaven.

The fifth hymn is a mythology of creation, of the fall of man, of Christ's story of redemption, and of the world's salvation. "The most childlike natures" flocked to Christ. They received their inner call to apostolic office. With these disciples and apostles mingles a "singer, born under serene skies of Hellas." The Greek is a representative of Hellenic art, and appears like an emissary of Apollo, a figure resembling Orpheus. He opens his heart to the new revelation in Palestine, for he recognizes in Christ the youthful form that embodies death on the tombs of Greece. But Christ is no longer the man of the "grim mask." He is the liberator, the victor over death's power. Thus the bard chants: "Der Jüngling bist du, der seit langer Zeit / Auf unsern Gräbern steht in tiefem Sinnen; / Ein tröstlich Zeichen in der Dunkelheit -/ Der höhern Menschheit freudiges Beginnen. / Was uns gesenkt in tiefe Traurigkeit, / Zieht uns mit süsser Sehnsucht nun von hinnen. / Im Tode ward das ewge Leben kund, / Du bist der Tod und machst uns erst gesund."

The bard goes to "Hindustan," bringing the glad tidings to the Far East, where soon after his departure, "the precious life became a sacrifice for fallen Man." It is the passion, death and resurrection of Christ that form the content of the remaining lines of the hymn.

This Greek bard is a mysterious figure. He is given no name. He can be traced to no literary model. He suddenly appears in the fifth hymn, in the middle of the story of redemption, only to vanish again without further mention. He comes from Hellas to Palestine, consecrates himself to the new divine revelation and passes on to India to proclaim the tidings.

In the twelfth chapter of the Gospel according to St. John, immediately after the resurrection of Lazarus and prior to the Passion, there is mention of "certain Greeks . . . that came up (to Jerusalem) to worship at the feast." When Christ heard of their arrival, he exclaimed: "The hour is come, that the Son of man should be glorified" (St. John, 12: 23). The fifth hymn describes precisely this juncture before the Passion. More than that, the words of the twelfth chapter of the Gospel of St. John have Christ say: "He that loveth his life shall lose it; and he that hateth his life in this world shall keep it unto life eternal. If any man serve me, let him follow me; and where I am, there shall also my servant be" (St. John, 12:25/26).

The bard is such a servant, following Christ. He no longer clings to life in the sense of the pagan, who fears death. What he sees in Christ is this:

> In Death eternal life at last was found,
> Thyself art Death, 'tis thou doth make us sound.

The bard from Hellas is none other than the epitome of the poet, the herald of Orpheus. There is a significant fragment that entitles us to such a view. "The reconciliation of the Christian with the pagan religion. The story of Orpheus, Psyche, etc."

The fifth hymn describes this "reconciliation of the Christian with the pagan religion." But in a deeper sense the story of Orpheus is the transfiguration of the poet as such. The myth of Orpheus and Eurydice sings of the destiny of the primordial poet. It is the poem of poetry - Eurydice lost and regained. It is a theme that is at the very core of Novalis' own destiny.

The end of the fifth hymn is a chant of the Resurrection. The stone of the Sepulchre has been lifted - "Mankind is now arisen." "Mankind" here means the primordial human element, the First Man, the sum total of human qualities as the supreme idea. It is Christ, as the representative of mankind, the earth's own self. To understand correctly this last section of the hymn, which passes over altogether into the form of a "devotional song," we must discuss at greater length a theme already touched upon by Novalis in Klingsor's tale, a theme that recurs at the beginning of the fifth hymn. This is the mythical image of the flame. "All races as though children revered the tender, thousandfold flame as the highest in the world" we read at the beginning of the fifth hymn, in the description of life before the dawn of history as a "soaring, colorful festival of the children of Heaven and the denizens of Earth." Only the thought of death, which even the gods faced in perplexity, interrupted the feast of life.

Later on, this thousandfold flame is called "the soul of the world," and ultimately the "new world." Toward the end of the hymn it becomes "all the sun that lights us." The flame is Christ. It manifests the ancient "light" as Christ manifests God the Father. The flame is light and warmth. Light and warmth are the cosmic powers of love, and it is this love that kindles the flame, the divine spark in the individual self.

"The flame has come," sounds the call in Klingsor's tale, meaning that the "long night," frozen in ice, has come to an end and the Golden Age is about to return. It is of this ultimate state that the fifth hymn sings toward its end, a paean of the flame, of the Logos risen.

This flame is without, as well as within; cosmic light as well as human warmth. The resurrection applies not alone to mankind in general, but to the individual man. It is an event immanent in the self. In this connection, too, we find a fragment in the papers of Novalis that may serve as a helpful commentary: "About our self - as the flame of the body within the soul - similarity of the soul to oxygen. All synthesis is a flame or a spark, or some analogue of these." Man's self thus is an "analogue" of the flame, a spark from the "thousandfold flame" of the world. It is of this flame of the world as the essence of mankind that the poem at the end of the fifth hymn sings: "Zur Hochzeit ruft der Tod-/ Die Lampen brennen helle-/ Die Jungfraun sind zur Stelle-/ um Öl ist keine Not-/ . . . . . .Die Lieb' ist frei gegeben, / Und keine Trennung mehr. / Es wogt das volle Leben / Wie ein unendlich Meer. / Nur eine Nacht der Wonne-/ Ein ewiges Gedicht-/ Und unser aller Sonne / Ist Gottes Angesicht."

Death, calling to the marriage, is Christ who vanquished death by His Resurrection. This marriage is the *unio sacra* of the mystics, the "chymical marriage" of the alchemists, a goal in the growth of the soul toward which all men may aspire.

The paean of the Resurrection passes directly into the sixth and last hymn, which bears the heading "Yearning for Death," a title probably introduced into print by Schlegel without the poet's knowledge and mistakenly transposed from a note applied to the fourth hymn. This sixth hymn carries forward the apocalyptic vision of the future. It is the song of the return to the Father. "The days of yore" - three times in three successive stanzas these words are sounded - the time for the return has come, when we shall be bound for home, where we shall again find what we lost in the days of yore - the essence of light heralded at the beginning of the first hymn.

If the words "O! sauge, Geliebter, gewaltig mich an" at the end of the fourth hymn were a wishful prayer of prophetic vision, then the words: "Hinunter zu der süssen Braut, / Zu Jesus dem Geliebten -/" at the end of the whole work imply the fulfillment of the return to the "Father's heart" as perfect children of God. "Ein Traum bricht unsre Banden los / Und senkt uns in des Vaters Schoss."

Now that we have surveyed the work, let us look at the inner structure of the composition as a whole.

The first hymn states the anxious question: "What if the Light never returned to its children?" The last hymn replies: "We must repair to the heavenly place," we sink on the "Father's heart." The themes of the first and last hymns correspond like question and answer.

Just as the first hymn corresponds to the last, so does the second to the poem included at the end of the fifth - though in form and content it stands on its own. There we have the power of sleep, here that of the Resurrection; there the silent messenger of the unconscious power of creative life, here the soul's awakening into superconscious life; there life-filled sensuousness in the almond tree's oil, the juice of the poppy, the maiden's bosom, here death calling to the marriage, the transfiguration - "the star-world now is flowing as living golden wine."

The third hymn again, like the first, is held in the first person. It gives voice to personal experience in utterly individual terms. Compare these lines spoken from the innermost human self with the content of the fifth hymn (excluding the Resurrection paean), which tells the whole myth of creation and the story of mankind. No greater contrast can be imagined. On the one hand is the most highly individual expression of the death of Sophia; on the other the historic turning-point of Christ at Golgotha. First the words come from the poet's own self; then from the epitome of the poet, in historical and mythical personification, as the bard from Hellas.

The fourth hymn has no counterpart; it is the heart of the work, the inner balance-wheel. However the stanza at its conclusion appears as the middle of the middle: it carries over the mystery of Sophia, already touched upon in the preceding hymn, and paves the way for the vision of Christ heralded in the next two.

Thus the internal structure falls into seven stages. The numbering of the six hymns is of no consequence. The manuscript actually shows notes, in free verse, for another hymn (between the fourth and the fifth), and it seems plausible to believe that the poet would have inserted this hymn into the work and perhaps altogether changed the numbering, had he been given more time. The keynote of the hymns is the path from the personal self to the experience of Christian communion, or in the words of Novalis' mythology: From Sophia to Christ.

Both as poetry and as fable, the *Hymns To The Night* have much in common with Klingsor's tale. Both works are pilgrimages, "homeward bound." But the tale still offers in terms of pagan nature mythology what the *Hymns* pour into the words and concepts of Christianity. In the tale, symbolism still shrouds what the *Hymns* reveal as the historic fact of redemption. Sophia, in the tale, keeps the mystery of the world, the flame. In the *Hymns*, the stone is lifted, the mystery of the Resurrection becomes manifest. In the tale, Sophia remains the priestess of the heart. The *Hymns* manifest the love of the Logos in the heart. The tale is to the *Hymns* what the bud is to the blossom. The ideas of the *Hymns* add up to a metamorphosis and enhancement of those of the tale - a fact that proves even better than critical manuscript study that the *Hymns* were written at a later date.

The first four hymns point the way to the experience of man's true self. The three last stages of the two hymns that follow represent something that transcends the individual self of man, as it rests within its divine matrix.

We may, therefore, look upon the *Hymns to the Night* as the document of a free, Christian poet. In the form of poetry it shows what the painters of yore in their cathedral pictures represented as the "Stations of the Cross." The fourth hymn, right down to individual word images, plainly takes the form of a "Bearing of the Cross," a pilgrimage to the Holy Sepulchre. The concluding poem of the fourth hymn reflects the death at Golgotha in individual formulation. The images of the fifth hymn trace the Sepulchre and Resurrection, and the sixth hymn is essentially an Ascension scene, for the keynote is not "Yearning for Death," as the title misleadingly puts it, but "Return to the Father."

The three hymns that make up the beginning of the work are intended to prepare us for these "Stations of the Cross." A keynote of melancholy is sounded in the first hymn, together with a note of humility in the face of night, whom the poet seeks to serve. As do light and night in the first hymn, so in the second, time and eternity face the seer's soul as crucial questions. "Must ever the morning return? Endeth never the thralldom of Earth?" Yearning for eternity is the title that might well have been given to this hymn.

The third hymn proceeds from space and time to the inward life of man, to the depths of consciousness. Fear of solitude precedes the inner rebirth, an ordeal the soul must withstand before it can relive the Passion, experience the Bearing of the Cross, the Death, the Sepulchre and the Resurrection as inward "mystic events."

Thus we reach seven stages in the structure of the work. The end returns to the beginning. But in the end the beginning is enhanced. Light returns, but its return opens up a realm of grace never before seen. The mystic union is achieved, for Christ has become Lord of the Earth.

The reading of English mystical poetry like that of Edward Young's *Night Thoughts* exerted but a peripheric influence. The *Hymns* stand alone in European poetry through their genuine spontaneity of artistic conception. To be sure, not all parts of this cycle of poems are equally transparent in form and content. The rhythmical prose within the first two hymns is sometimes ponderous. The third hymn reveals the greatest spontaneity, but only the rhymed verses within the fourth, fifth and sixth hymns attain completely unaffected simplicity which is so characteristic of the *Devotional Songs* later on.

The structure of the whole composition does not as yet reveal full mastery of inner balance. In terms of length the fifth hymn is equal to the sum of the four that precede it. The picture of antiquity which Novalis offers reminds us of Schiller's *The Gods of Greece,* although it goes beyond this poem which mourns the decline of the ancient gods while Novalis made the advent of Christ the turning-point.

We also find in the manuscript version several words set down which are put in parentheses and are surely notes in the conception of another hymn that remained unwritten. This is further evidence that the composition of this cycle did not mature to that degree of perfection the poet wanted to attain. This seems to be particularly true in regard to the external numbering of the six hymns which reveal inwardly a sevenfold structure. The last verse of the fifth hymn reaches a height to which the sixth hymn appears as a slight anticlimax. This fact gives reason to doubt that the last hymn was actually intended as part of the cycle.

In spite of these shortcomings, there is a magic spell which made the hymns famous from the very beginning up to modern revivals in English, French and Russian translations. The reality of Novalis' mystical insight seems to be undeniable. To doubt the fact of his inspiration would mean to pass damning judgment on the authenticity of his poetic gift. To envision him but as a rambling dreamer, a dilettante poet, could never explain the impact of his work, let alone the fact that soon after his death, when he was still virtually unknown, several of his poems entered the popular hymnals of the Protestant churches and became almost like folksongs. This is especially true of the cycle of poems written simultaneously with the last version of the hymns and immediately after, his *Devotional Songs*.

7. DEVOTIONAL SONGS

The *Hymns to the Night* seem to recall the hour of the individual's day of awakening. The *Devotional Songs*, on the other hand, sing of the common festivals of the year.

Novalis called the poems "Christian Songs." Their publication in the *Athenaeum* never came about, but he intended there to title them "Specimens From a New Devotional Songbook." After the death of Novalis Friedrich Schlegel and Ludwig Tieck took one word from each of these two designations and published the poems in his collected works under the title "Devotional Songs."

The strangely moving element in these "Songs" is the immediacy with which the poet sings of the events of the holy story, as though he had witnessed them in the flesh. He once noted: "In gatherings for the worship of God, each member should rise and tell the others divine stories from the wealth of his own experience. Such religious heed to sunny glimpses into the other world is a main requirement of religious man." It was such "sunny glimpses into the other world" that Novalis sought to communicate in the *Devotional Songs*. They were to be spiritual spadework in the founding of a new poetic form of Christianity rather than a mere continuation of Lutheran church song or the Pietist congregational chant, or mere imitation of the Catholic "Songs of Mary."

His idea of a "poetic Christianity" sprang from no esthetic abstraction. The religious character of Novalis was that of a reformer. He was a Protestant, but neither Lutheranism nor

Pietism correspond to his ideal of Christianity to come. "The Pietists sought to introduce the spirit of childhood. But is it the true spirit of childhood? Is it not rather the child-mother spirit, the old-woman spirit? When Christ said "Become like unto little children" he meant real children—not spoiled, coddled, sugary children. This spirit of childhood is the essence of his poetic creativeness. It is the source of his passage about the "humble poetic abode" where the birth of Christ took place, "infinite fruit of mysterious embrace."

The very first of the *Devotional Songs*, titled "Without Him and With Him," is a song in the "spirit of childhood," a poem of the advent. "Was wär ich ohne dich gewesen?/ Was würd' ich ohne dich nicht sein?/Zu Furcht und Ängsten auserlesen,/Ständ' ich in weiter Welt allein./ Nichts wüsst' ich sicher, was ich liebte,/ Die Zukunft wär ein dunkler Schlund;/ Und wenn mein Herz sich tief betrübte,/ Wem tät' ich meine Sorge kund?"

The song consists of ten eight-line iambic stanzas and its structure reveals an important feature. There is a clear distinction between the first four stanzas, in which the pronoun "I" is dominant, and the last five, in which "we" appears without exception. The fifth stanza, marking the turning-point from "I" to "we", speaks in the second person plural. To the "I" that starts out by asking: "Was wär ich ohne dich gewesen?" Christ reveals Himself, and only thereby is the "I" truly born. This birth of the self takes place in the consciousness of the true spirit of childhood: "Für alle seine tausend Gaben/ Bleib ich sein demutvolles Kind,/ Gewiss ihn unter uns zu haben,/ Wenn zwei auch nur versammelt sind./"

This end of the fourth stanza is the core of the whole poem. The self becomes the humble child of Christ. This is no longer the individual self with its sensibility, melancholy, self-reflection and vanity, but the new-born self of the Christian flock.

The last two stanzas close with an apocalyptic vision of a state to come when there shall be no more sin, since all men have become children of God. Christ appears as "heiliger Geliebter" living in wondrous glory, the sanctifying power of love.

The first "Song" closes on the image that every man received into the heart of Christ ripens as the fruit of Paradise.

It is of this Garden of Eden that the second "Song" tells—though it is customarily called a Christmas song. These designations, however, must not be used as a straitjacket to interpretation. The "Song" says nothing of the shepherds at the manger, of the humble stable, of the winter night's promise. It presents a cosmic fact: the birth of Christ is an event of nature here on earth. Written in trochaic cadence, the poem manifests, down to the sounds of the words, the descent of the Word of God to the realm of man. The divine Word, the *Logos,* is first exalted as the "holy child." "Endlich kommt zur Erde nieder/ Aller Himmel selges Kind." It is He who brings peace forever, standing with full hands in the center of mankind. Finally He is shown as the spirit of the earth, joining the seasons, uniting all the cardinal points of the world: "Unser ist sie nun geworden,/ Gottheit, die uns oft erschreckt,/ Hat im Süden und im Norden/ Himmelskeime rasch geweckt./ Und so lasst im vollen Gottesgarten/ Treu uns jede Knosp' und Blüte warten."

Poetically, this song is more mature than the first. The first clung to a tone of preachment, but the second revels in bold, tangible sense images that are without peer. None of the traditional sentimentality about the "sweet little Jesus child" is to be found. The "Child of Heaven" is no metaphor; it is the expression of a worldly event. It plunges into "life's foaming flood," about which "breathes awakening bloom." The Godhead which oft dismayed us—the Jehovah of the Old Testament—here He has become our own and the Garden of Eden awaits us here on earth. Here in the song the sensible-supersensible immediacy of the mystic is coupled with the devout dignity of the evangelist who moralizes no longer, since "worldly and heavenly" have become one. There is nothing left to lament, no dirge of penitence. The aphorisms of the thinker have been redeemed by the creative poet.

The cosmic vision that encompasses Christ as the spirit of the earth is not immediately continued in the songs that follow. It returns only in the seventh poem, the "Hymn." The third, fourth, fifth and sixth songs come from the poet's self. The self, however, is one that has passed through the "we" of the Christian congregation. The precise time at which these songs were composed has not been established, and it is unlikely that they were written in the presently accepted sequence. Yet there is significance in the fact that Novalis desired to publish them in this sequence, or thus assembled them in manuscript.

In the third song we hear the poet cry out: "Ich fall' ihm weinend in die Arme:/ Auch mir war einst, wie dir zumut." This "thee" is addressed to the man who still faces the awakening at the hands of Christ. This recurrent "who" in such lines as "Wer einsam sitzt in seiner Kammer" or "Wem nur gefärbt von Not und Jammer" is the Old Adam, the self before rebirth, a rebirth sharply highlighted at the heart of the poem: "Mit ihm kommt neues Blut und Leben/ In dein erstorbenes Gebein—/ Und wenn du ihm dein Herz gegeben,/ So ist auch seines ewig dein."

If the third song is still tinged with melancholy and sorrow, together with a certain note of preachment, the fourth bespeaks the pure joy of certainty in the Resurrection. The lifting of the stone is an outward as well as an inward event. To the mystic it is the symbol of the awakening, the keynote of the rebirth, "Christ and Sophia," though no names are mentioned: "Da ich so im stillen krankte,/ Ewig weint' und wegverlangte,/ Und nur blieb vor Angst und Wahn:/ Ward mir plötzlich wie von oben/ Weg des Grabes Stein gehoben,/ Und mein Innres aufgetan./ Wen ich sah, und wen an seiner/ Hand erblickte, frage keiner,/ ....."

More than twenty times the fifth song has been set to music by noted composers, including Franz Schubert. It is one of Novalis' best-known poems, among the first that entered the church hymnals. It begins on an anapaestic measure that heightens the feeling of humility and endearment. The mood of supplication sets off the utter simplicity and inwardness of the poem. It is a vow of fealty. Inward leads the pilgrimage, from day to night. In the last stanza the sevenfold conditional "if" in "Wenn ich ihn nur habe" becomes the "where" of certainty: "Wo ich ihn nur habe,/ Ist mein Vaterland."

These poems are the experiences of a mystic, but they are expressed in inimitably simple language, in terms familiar to the popular tongue, in rhythm and tone that invite us to sing. The symbols of fantasy, the metaphors of the *Hymns*—they have all vanished. In choice of words and images the Songs chant an air so simple that any mind may receive it. Indeed, so much did they take on a life of their own, quite apart from their creator, that not very long after his death certain minor changes were made. There were many efforts at variation and imitation, but even the formal skill of Tieck could not approach the poetic genuineness of a poem like the sixth song: "Wenn alle untreu werden,/ So bleib' ich dir doch treu;/ Dass Dankbarkeit auf Erden/ Nicht ausgestorben sei./ Für mich umfing dich Leiden,/ Vergingst für mich in Schmerz;/ Drum geb ich dir mit Freuden/ Auf ewig dieses Herz."

Despite impure and commonplace rhymes, we cannot escape

the feeling that the soul of a peerless poet opens up to us here, that his words stem truly from the heart of an artist. The keynote of faith is neither sentimental nor grandiloquent, for behind the simplicity of the verses lies the power of mystic experience.

This becomes manifest once again in the "Hymn" which Novalis put in seventh place among his *Devotional Songs*. It appears like an inner sun within the system of the whole collection.

The keynote of the "Hymn" involves the mystery of the Holy Communion. Even in the fifth *Hymn to the Night* he chanted of the "Golden Grail" before which "all bitter sorrow fades." The same theme dominates the "Hymn." The hymn of the Sacrament becomes a chant of the world's golden end. But Christ represents not merely the power of love as the world's highest communion, He is the Beloved, to be cherished by all men in free consciousness. It is from this knowledge that flow the exalted lines: "Wer kann sagen,/ Dass er das Blut versteht?/ Einst ist alles Leib,/ Ein Leib,/ In himmlischem Blute/ Schwimmt das selige Paar.—/ O! dass das Weltmeer/ Schon errötete,/ Und in duftiges Fleisch/ Aufquölle der Fels!"

Like a jewel shining with a quiet glow the "Hymn" nestles among the colorful fragrance of the *Songs*. The *Songs* as a whole reveal the faith of the earthbound self in Christ. But the "Hymn" tears open the worldly background of love. It stands between the sixth and eighth songs as does the Passion between Christmas and Easter. It is, as it were, a hymn of Maundy Thursday, necessarily followed by the lamentation of Good Friday.

The eighth song is this lament in the Good Friday mood, put in the mouth of Mary Magdalene. Once again, with the full power of emotion, it expresses the loneliness of the self that has not yet fused with the mystery of the Sacrament. It is the anxious expectation of Easter Morn, not yet followed by fulfillment: "Weinen muss ich, immer weinen;/ Möcht' er einmal nur erscheinen,/ Einmal nur von ferne mir," thus the song begins and culminates in the fifth stanza: "Nirgends kann ich hier auf Erden/ Jemals wieder glücklich werden,/ Alles ist ein düstrer Traum./ Ich bin auch mit ihm verschieden,/ Läg' ich doch mit ihm in Frieden/ Schon im unterirdschen Raum."

This anxious lament of the Passion Week, written in the trochaic mood, is followed by a triumphant Easter song in iambic cadences, a Resurrection chant full of jubilation without bounds. This song shines like the dawn of Easter Sunday after the dark night of Good Friday. The individual self has awakened to the sunlike certainty of the Resurrection that calls to the flock: "Ich sag' es jedem, dass er lebt/ Und auferstanden ist,/ Dass er in unsrer Mitte schwebt/ Und ewig bei uns ist." The Resurrection is not merely a fact to man but to all earth. Thus the song closes on the image of a "world renewed to life"—which is the true meaning of the Easter Day: "Er lebt, und wird nun bei uns sein,/ Wenn alles uns verlässt!/ Und so soll dieser Tag uns sein/ Ein Weltverjüngungsfest."

These nine poems, from the song of Advent to the chant of the Resurrection, form an inner cycle—a year of the Christian soul. With the Easter song of the Resurrection a climax is reached— an unsurpassable climax pointing into the future of the earth for all time to come. The Golden Age is no longer the symbolic aptheosis of a fantasy, of philosophical dialectic, the metaphor of moral preachment or demand. No, the Resurrection marked its actual beginning. We ourselves partake of it, to the measure and power of our consciousness. Surely this does not mean, in the sense of Novalis, that we are to become "prophets." The mystery of the Resurrection, rather has supplied the impulse that may save the world from petrification, mankind from decline. In his own life a Godlike man sets an example of what the goal of earthly man may be in the dim future—to do deeds of purest love in utter freedom. It is in this impulse for the future that the meaning of a "Weltverjüngungsfest" lies.

The songs that follow in the collection were added either by the poet or by his editors. They continue the pilgrimage at lofty heights, but they ascend no new peaks. The tenth poem is a song of the Cross. It was originally written on the same sheet with Klingsor's songs, intended for *Heinrich von Ofterdingen,* the background of which we shall discuss further on. Significantly enough, the sixth stanza of this Song of the Cross says: "Geh zu dem Wunderstamme,/ Gib stiller Sehnsucht Raum,/ Aus ihm geht eine Flamme/ Und zehrt den schweren Traum."

The tree of wonder (*Wunderstamm*) is the Cross—but it is not mere dead wood. It is part of the "Tree of Life," from the timber of which, according to ancient legend, the Cross of Golgotha was cut. From this wood, the legendary remnant of Paradise, issues a "flame." This familiar theme of the flame from Klingsor's tale is again put into the mouth of the bard in *Heinrich von Ofterdingen.*

The eleventh song is a rhymed sermon, directly influenced by Schleiermacher's *Discourses*. The six middle stanzas appear like a single rhetorical question put by the preacher to his flock. But ultimately the tone of preachment passes into surrender to the "Helden der Liebe:" "Nimm Du mich hin, du Held der Liebe!/ Du bist mein Leben, meine Welt." In language and content this poem is less warm and intimate. The didactic tone of preachment outweighs the original poetic element. A few phrases border on the commonplace, seem almost borrowed from traditional church song.

The twelfth song, regarded as a poem of Whitsuntide, took over almost verbatim several verses and images, as well as its whole structure, from a Catholic Song Book dating back to the year 1631. Thus it is not an original creation. Actually it is not a song of Whitsuntide at all. It exalts the Epiphany of Christ— the baptism in the River Jordan, celebrated on January 6. "Der Winter weicht, ein neues Jahr/ Steht an der Krippe Hochaltar./ Es ist das erste Jahr der Welt/ Die sich dies Kind erst selbst bestellt."

This is praise to the descent of the Son of God, uttered as a cosmic event. The universe—nature, earth, the starry sky—seek to receive the Son of God, to give Him shelter. In this very poem, following an already existing model, comparison clearly shows how Novalis' poetic genius of language was able to transmute the most brittle and commonplace material into lofty art. Let us compare just one passage from Novalis' poem with literal precedents in the Catholic songbook of Father Gregory Corner:

Corner:	Novalis:
"O klare Sonn, du schöner Stern	"Er ist der Stern, er ist die Sonn',
dich wollten wir anschauen gern."	Er ist des ewgen Lebens Bronn.
	Aus Kraut und Stein und Meer und Licht
	Schimmert sein kindlich Angesicht."

The thirteenth song was conceived at the time of Novalis' mortal illness and bears the character of a personal prayer, a "Gethsemane" of individual suffering. The two poems that follow are entitled "Songs of Mary" and speak in the innermost voice of which Novalis was capable. He turns to Mary as though he were addressing his own mother in childlike humility. He begs the "sweet Mother" to give him a sign. In his dreams he sees her with the "infant God in arms" who "takes pity on his playmate," the boy who later became St. John the Baptist. He sings as though he himself directly sought to recall the Bible Age. Never before had Novalis written verse with such an intimacy. The mood of humility rules out every tinge of vanity or conceit. Here he pleads indeed for the "true spirit of childhood:" "Kindlich berühr ich deinen Saum/ Erwecke mich aus diesem schweren Traum," and in the end he begs the Mother: "Mache mich zu deinem Kinde."

This is one of the fundamental motifs of all Novalis' work. It sounds in the *Novices* and in Klingsor's tale—"Within each dwells the Heavenly Mother, to give birth to each child forevermore." We find it again in the aphorisms on the Sistine Madonna, where we read: "As a child the spirit of poetry may have looked like the angel below the Madonna, pressing his finger to his mouth in significant gesture." These themes fuse with his ideal of poetic Christianity, a creed that is all art and an art that stems from a deeper knowledge of the world. All this is expressed in the two "Songs of Mary," personally and at once superpersonally, artlessly and at once from the depths of knowledge, mysteriously and at once with the utter simplicity of folksong. "Unzähligmal standst du bei mir/ Mit Kindeslust sah ich nach dir,/ Dein Kindlein gab mir seine Hände,/ Dass es dereinst mich wieder fände;/ Du lächeltest voll Zärtlichkeit/ Und küsstest mich, o himmelsüsse Zeit!".

The fifteenth and last song, though written on the same sheet with Klingsor's songs for *Heinrich von Ofterdingen*, carries on the mood of the first "Song of Mary," concluding the collection. The thousand likenesses of the Madonna painted by the masters of the middle ages and the Renaissance, though they may have flown with richness from the world of faith, are as naught to Novalis when compared to the image before the soul's own vision. The vision of the Madonna is the goal of his path as a poet with all its turns and metamorphoses. This juncture at which his soul saw what none of the paintings could depict leads us back to the heart of his life. After all the metamorphoses that attended his way from the *Novices* and Klingsor's tale to the *Hymns to the Night* and the *Devotional Songs,* the last gossamer veil seems to be lifted from the image at Sais in this miniature portrait at the end of the cycle. "Ich sehe dich in tausend Bildern,/ Maria, lieblich ausgedrückt,/Doch keins von allen kann dich schildern,/ Wie meine Seele dich erblickt./ —Ich weiss nur, dass der Welt Getümmel/ Seitdem mir wie ein Traum verweht,/ Und ein unnennbar süsser Himmel/ Mir ewig im Gemüte steht."

When we look in conclusion at the structure of the whole collection, it becomes noteworthy that but once, in the first song, is the name of Christ mentioned, and but once, in the last, that of Mary. The sequence of these poems soars as though on a golden bridge across a stream where on one bank rests the mystery of the Son, while the other shelters the secret of the Virgin. To Novalis Christ is the "Beloved," the "Savior," the "Son of Man," the "Liberator," the "Child of Heaven," the "Godhead," the "Lord," "He," the "Dear Being," "Lofty Child of Fairest Mother," the "Infant God," 'Love's Hero," "Earth's Consolation," "Star," "Sun," "Life's fount that evermore will run." To him Mary is the Mother—"Mother fair," "Sweet Mother," the "Virgin," the "Blessed Queen," "Queen of my Heart."

The *Hymns to the Night* lead from the maternal matrix of the world, from the night, from Sophia, to the risen Christ, whereas the *Devotional Songs* lead from Christ to Mary-Sophia. The *Hymns* are inspired by Sophia and guide the poet to Christ. The *Songs* transfigure the earthly image of Sophia into that of the heavenly queen of the world, by the light of Christ.

"He read some Christian songs to us as well," Friedrich Schlegel wrote to Schleiermacher. "They are the most sublime he has ever written. Their poetry resembles nothing, except the most deep-felt of Goethe's earlier, shorter poems." Schleiermacher himself called the *Songs* an example of "devout poetry in all its power and glory." Half a century later Wilhelm Dilthey exclaimed: "Like Christianity, these songs will live forever."

The *Devotional Songs* are an effort at "poetic Christianity" as a synthesis of early Christian and Protestant-Pietistic forces. This may explain the singular fact that only seven years after the poet's death (1808) several of the *Songs* (the first, third, fourth, fifth, sixth and ninth) were taken into the Bergen songbook; later, through Schleiermacher's influence, into the Berlin hymnal; and still later, with occasional slight modifications, as though they came from the ancient treasure of folklore, into the churchbooks of Mecklenburg, Württemberg, Rhineland, Hanover, Minden, and finally into Protestant hymnals all over the world.

The power that made it possible for poetry of so individualistic a lyricist to become popular church song can be explained only by the simplicity of word and image, created from the profundity of the poet's heart.

8. CHRISTENDOM OR EUROPE

During the fall of 1799 Novalis wrote his essay *Christendom or Europe* and in mid-November he read it to his friends at Jena. From the first moment, the work aroused passionate differences of opinion. Nothing that he had written before met such determined resistance. The essay was omitted altogether from the first editions of his writings. Not until a quarter-century after his death did Schlegel himself publish it, without the knowledge of Tieck, who again excluded it from subsequent editions. An English translation, however, was published in London in 1844. In Germany it was finally reprinted in the last third of the nineteenth century and included in each of the rapidly following editions of his works. Our own century has long since counted this essay among the central works of Novalis.

Christendom or Europe carries a threefold symbolism: it stands as a tragic document bespeaking the loneliness of a poet's mission, as a somber hieroglyph in the literature of the turn of the eighteenth century, and as the foreboding herald of the break-up and disintegration of early Romanticism.

His thoughts at the core of this exalted oration take us back a decade. At the age of eighteen under the influence of Schiller's historical studies and Herder's ideas, Novalis had embodied the fruits of his reading in the draft of an essay he called *Sketches for a Philosophy of the History of Mankind.* He had signed the still immature product with the pen-name of Friedrich Waller. Ten years later he exclaimed: "In his presentation the historian must be an orator. It is gospels he is proffering—for all history is a gospel."

It must, therefore, be kept in mind from the outset that the work of the former Schiller student merely appears to be an essay on the philosophy of history. Yet in essence it is a religious sermon, taking on the form of a prose hymn in its structure and word music.

Its content was conditioned by the events in Europe which took on world significance about the turn of the century. Novalis had taken a deep interest in the French Revolution from its very outset. The turmoil of the National Assembly; the assault on the

Tuileries; the fall of the monarchy; the execution of Louis XVI and Marie Antoinette; the coalition campaign against the French Republic, leading to world war with England, Spain, Portugal, the Italian and German states and Austria; the Jacobin reign of terror; Danton, Marat, Robespierre; the declaration of the Convention to celebrate the Festival of Reason at the Cathedral of Notre Dame in Paris, with the proclamation that the time had come to destroy religion since mankind had put aside its swaddling clothes—all these fateful and world-shaking events formed the background to Novalis' own youth.

He was a student at Leipzig when Goethe, accompanying the Duke of Weimar during the campaign in France, said on the night of the cannonade at Valmy: "Here and today a new era of history has dawned." When in 1795 his kinsman, Minister of State von Hardenberg, concluded the Peace of Basle with France, Novalis was a law clerk at Tennstedt and already secretly engaged to Sophia. After she had died, General Bonaparte, in the wake of brief victories in Italy, rose to European renown through bloody exploits, and Pope Pius VI, captured by his troops, submitted to the peace treaty of Tolentino. While Novalis was writing his *Novices at Sais*, Napoleon was fighting in the shadow of the Pyramids. At the time, finally, when Novalis was reading his essay to friends at Jena, Paris witnessed the "coup d'état" that named Napoleon First Consul—the last stage on his way to becoming world monarch. A renewed outbreak of devastating European warfare was imminent. England and Austria rejected Napoleon's peace offer, and he forthwith undertook his famous crossing of the Alps, invading Lombardy.

The background of this age must be kept in mind if Novalis' historical and philosophical oration is to be properly understood. Time and again he put down in his notebooks what seemed essential to him in grasping current political events. There are thoughts on monarchy, hierarchy, government by individuals, by representative constitution, by episcopal constitution, by aristocracy and by democracy; thoughts on the "tragic form of Primitive Christianity," on the spirit of chivalry in the crusades in which Europe became "visible," on the "treatment of history as gospel."

Since "all history is gospel," the historian must become an orator. His discourse must be a sermon. Here Novalis was again the disciple of Schiller, whose mind was akin to his own. In discussing the fifth "Hymn to the Night" we pointed out the parallel with Schiller's "Gods of Greece." We must look to this hymn as the germ and core of the thoughts that recur in changed and enhanced form in *Christendom or Europe*.

The essay appears like a vessel into which flowed waters from many currents and streams. Veneration for Schiller's vision, surrender to the ideas of Herder, Lessing's *Education of Mankind*, Schleiermacher's *Discourses*, the study of Church history dating back to the Wittenberg days, his dream of an encyclopedia and a new Bible, history as fable, fable as fairytale, the tale as a prophetic representation of the apocalypse, the love of the Middle Ages that pervaded the preparatory work for *Heinrich von Ofterdingen*—all this was cast in the form of a living exhortation to the existing reality at the turn of the century, against the background of Europe's unrest, with a foreboding of the abyss from which the tyrant threatened to rise to put Germany's freedom in thrall.

Lessing's final work, *The Education of Mankind* (1780) exercised a decisive effect similar to that of Schleiermacher's *Discourses* on Novalis' apocalyptic vision of the future. A few of Novalis' notes in the collection of fragments dating from his last years (1799-1800) show that he had reverted to the study of Lessing's work at this time: "The Gospels contain the outlines of higher gospels yet to come . . . mysteries of Christianity." In Lessing's book Novalis could read: "It surely will come—that time of fulfillment, when man's reason will feel more and more convinced of a better future, yet, in keeping with that conviction, will feel no need to borrow motives for his actions from that future. He will do good for its own sake, not because attached to it are arbitrary rewards, once merely calculated to fix and strengthen his fickle attention, that he might come to recognize the inner and better rewards on their own. It will surely come— that time of a *new and everlasting gospel* vouchsafed to us in the elementary scriptures of the New Covenant themselves."

Lessing here followed the eschatological ideas of Gioacchino da Fiore and other minds of the thirteenth and fourteenth centuries. This idea of a Third Age—that of the Holy Ghost, in Lessing's sense (since "the New Covenant must become as antiquated as the Old is now")—combined with the notion of a new gospel, forms the keynote of Novalis' essay.

The intimate relationship with Schleiermacher's *Discourses*, evident from the correspondence, has been greatly and one-sidedly overestimated, at the expense of Lessing's work. Schleiermacher, too, speaks of a Christianity of the future, insolubly bound up with the ideals of beauty and love inherent in a creative and therefore truly poetic spirit.

In close spiritual kinship with Novalis Schleiermacher exclaims: "He who sees not wonders of his own ... within whom revelations of his own never rise ... who does not sense now and then that a divine spirit urges him on, that he speaks and acts on holy inspiration—that man has no religion." Schleiermacher developed an apocalyptic vision of a Christianity to come, especially in the third and fourth of his *Discourses* on the "Invisible Church as the City of God," and on "Laymen and Priests," where he exclaims: "Every man is a priest to the extent that he draws others unto himself and into the field he has staked out as his own."

The name Schleiermacher in German means "veil maker," and Novalis, in a delicate play upon words, called his spiritual friend a "brother" to whom he sought to lead his listeners, for he "has made a new veil for the Virgin." Novalis called him the "heartbeat of the new age," and it would seem indeed as though the same spirit of the time pulsed in the veins of these two men.

In studying the organization and structure of *Christendom or Europe,* one grows aware of a basic pattern similar to that of the *Hymns,* completed at about the same time. The essay unfolds in a sevenfold sequence.

The first section of the essay confronts us with the United Europe of primitive Christianity. No hint is given of a date, but the description intimates a world before the schism into a Western and Eastern Church (in the ninth century) and does not even mention the turmoil of the great migrations and their consequences (in the fifth and sixth centuries). In this "mythical" world of yore, the Pope was the vicar of Christ's world government. Rome was the true Jerusalem. The people of this ideal primitive Christianity still have but one Prince and a single guild, the priesthood. In their veneration of Virgin and Child they are invested with the true "sense of childhood." The ideal image of this *ecclesia* is timeless. The church depicted in the first section is neither Gothic cathedral nor Romanesque minster, nor early medieval basilica. Nor are Rome and Jerusalem mere geographic names. They are symbols from the Apocalypse. The faith of all men was "fair," and in all parts of the world they sought to "proclaim the gospel of life and to make the Kingdom of Heaven the single realm of this world." But mankind is "not yet ripe for this glorious Kingdom." It speaks of the end of the "sense of sanctity." Faith and love become knowledge and possession. It is here that Novalis develops his doctrine of historical metamorphosis. The withering of the fair flower of youth (faith and love) brings to maturity more robust fruit (knowledge and possession). "Nothing that ever took hold of history is fleeting. From countless transformations emerge ever new and richer forms. Christianity had at one time appeared in its full power and glory, and even its ruins prevailed until a new world inspiration will come . . . . the true hegemony of Rome had quietly ceased long before the violent insurrection." Thus the coming of the new religion depends on a new "world inspiration," a true Whitsuntide that makes the Second Coming of Christ a reality in accordance with the Holy Scripture.

On the whole Novalis developed an optimistic concept of evolution. From the aspect of a higher order, every decline offers the chance for a new rise. This evolutionary idea leads us into the third section, the "third epistle" of historical vision. This section describes the Reformation and Counter-Reformation. Luther's important achievement became the tragic plaything of politics. Instead of the peace of Christendom there came the Wars of Religion. The spirit of nationalism coupled with the literal-minded faith of Bible exegesis, turned the work of liberation into the shackles of dynastic policy. The new monastic order of the Jesuits that had set the Counter-Reformation in motion tried in vain to return to the ideal Christianity of the early Church that had been lost. It, too, ultimately sank into impotent slumber on the borders of Europe.

Novalis made a sharp distinction between Lutheranism and Protestantism. In Luther he saw a power that was at heart reactionary, combining literal faith in the Bible with Augustinianism, and robbing the Church of all mystery in the process. Protestantism, on the other hand, meant to him, a progressive movement, not averse to a new Christianity to come. The order mentioned in the third section is never named by Novalis, merely designated as the "mother of secret societies." He had in mind the prototype of orders based on the practices of secret societies and of the true monastic life of the early Church as a historic example of inner regeneration. Novalis pointed to the temporal impermanence of the Society of Jesus in the same way as to the vain efforts of Zinzendorf and Boehme to found all-embracing communities.

In the fourth section of his essay he delved into the immediate present, the turn of his century. The Enlightenment appears as a second Reformation, an apostasy from apostasy. Knowledge and faith are utterly sundered and at odds. The prevailing mood is that of the end of the world. The sense of man has quite turned away from God. Man, once created in the image of God, is now shaped by the power of the machine. The universe is like a clattering mill, running idle, without a miller. God has become the idle spectator at a spectacle written by the sages of Enlightenment. The "philanthropists" and enlighteners rise as the new European "guild," supplanting the priesthood of former times.

Here the turning-point has been reached—the middle of the sevenfold structure. As this void is traversed, the beginnings of a new universe awaken. Just as in the fourth "Hymn" death becomes new life, so in *Christendom or Europe* the poet sweeps us away from the grave into the labor pains of a new birth. It is here that sermon passes into vision. The poet becomes herald and his images grow like those of the writer of the Apocalypse, who saw "in the midst of the seven candlesticks one like unto the Son of man . . . and his eyes were as a flame of fire . . . his voice as the sound of many waters . . . and his countenance was as the sun shineth in his strength" (Rev. I: 13-16).

Here, at the core of the essay, the turning-point in its downward sweep, we hear Novalis expostulate on the "fearful phenomenon of the modern age." In the "history of modern unbelief" he sees the key that can bring us back from hell to heaven: "A historically disposed mind can have no doubt that the time of resurrection has come, that the very events seemingly turned against its revival, and threatening to seal its doom, have become the most favorable auguries for its regeneration. True anarchy is the element in which religion is kindled. From the destruction of all that is positive, it lifts its glorious countenance as the founder of the new world. As though by his own power, man rises heavenward when he has no further ties . . . The spirit of God hovers above the waters, and as the waves sweep back, a heavenly isle becomes visible as the abode of the new man, as the watershed of life everlasting."

What does this language mean? "A heavenly isle as the abode of the new man"—"the spirit of God hovers above the waters"! These word images recall three primal stages in the history of mankind. The first stage is the beginning of creation, for in the First Book of Moses, Genesis, we read: "And the Spirit of God moved upon the face of the waters." The second stage is the Deluge—the survival of Noah and the new race that stemmed from him. The third stage is the historic turning-point that began with the baptism in the Jordan: "And Jesus, when he was baptized, went up straightway out of the water: and, lo, the heavens were opened unto him, and he saw the Spirit of God descending like a dove, and lighting upon him" (Matthew 3:16).

Chaos and beginning! From the darkness shines the creation of the world—such is the shifting spectacle, ever repeated for the salvation of mankind. As the rainbow arched in the sky for Noah after the Deluge, a sign of the Covenant between God and mankind, so after the twilight of the ancient gods and the decline of antiquity the New Covenant with God was concluded, beginning with the baptism in the Jordan.

Up to this point the contents, images, and words of the essay show that it is an historical study in the philosophy of religion. Beyond this point it becomes a personal preachment. For in the very first paragraph of the fifth section the poet's own self speaks in tones of immediate and individual address: "It is to history I would refer you. Delve into its instructive interrelations for similar junctures in time, and learn to employ the magic wand of analogy."

"The magic wand of analogy"—that is what Novalis challenges us to employ. Hence our reference to Deluge and atonement, to original sin and baptism, is no mere empty metaphor. But for this magic wand we grope as though in a void, when we seek to interpret the second half of the essay. For there all is vision of a world not yet in existence, prophecy of a state not yet come, a hymn of hope not yet fulfilled. Yet those very sections are directed toward the immediate present. The preacher calls to his flock —not a random flock somewhere in the world or in Europe, but in Germany, his own country. He calls out to his own nation: "Shall the Revolution remain French, as the Reformation was Lutheran? Is Protestantism once again to become unnaturally fixed in the form of revolutionary government? Is the "letter to make way but for another letter?" He implores the Germans: "Oh, that ye were filled with the spirit of spirits, that ye ceased this foolhardy endeavor to mold history and mankind, to give them your own image!" Prophetic words, that seem valid in the twentieth century even more than at the end of the eighteenth! Yet it is for the sake of these very words that the remaining part of the essay must not be misread as an expression of nationalistic instincts. They reveal visionary insight into the essence of German idealism. "In Germany traces of a new world can be discovered with full assurance. . . . The German is shaping himself into a fellow of a higher cultural epoch. . . . A matchless range and marvelous depth. . . . a powerful inkling of the unique sanctity and omnipotence of the soul of mankind seems to stir everywhere." The German element in this idealism is "universal individuality." It is cosmopolitan—"a new history, a new race of man." It is Europe. Hence the "historic vision" of the seer encompasses "the inmost conception of a new Messiah in its thousand facets all at once." This prophetic view heralds a "new Golden Age, the time of the great reconciliation, a savior who is truly at home among men, like a tutelary spirit."

The whole treatise is the pledge of a new spirit of religion. The way for it is paved by the erupting "universal spirit of cosmopolitan idealism" heralded for the first time in Germany.

The sixth section again leads us to an understanding of the German actuality at the turn of the century, using the "magic wand of analogy." As the gods of paganism were once redeemed by Christianity, so must the idols of Rationalism and the Enlightenment now give way to the light of new revelation. For "where there are no gods, specters prevail . . . and the time when the specters of Europe truly rose . . . was the period of transition from the mythology of the Greek gods to Christianity." Using the magic wand of analogy, we must recognize that the poet saw himself in historic perspective even in his own lifetime.

What Novalis seeks to do is to rally a new first flock. "Unto a brother shall I lead ye." The immediate image of this brother is Schleiermacher, the great exhorter of Berlin, whose name appears in the gentle and symbolic play upon words. Yet Schleiermacher himself is but a symbol for the new man as such: "This brother is the heartbeat of the new age. He who has felt it doubts its coming no more and goes with sweet pride as a witness . . . to join the flock of disciples." The image of this new flock of disciples again suggests an analogy with the followers of the Baptist, especially when one reads the following lines, spoken in the highly individualized first person, like a call to a new founding rally: "To me it is no more than the solemn call to a new founding rally, the mighty wing-beat of a passing angelic herald. These are the first pangs of labor. Let each prepare himself for the birth!"

This is the second passage to sound immediately from the exhorter's self. The first time, Novalis had merely pointed to the magic wand of analogy. Now he himself, with his call for a new founding rally, effects a historic analogy. The preacher calls the enlighteners and encyclopedists into the "lodge" that establishes peace.

The sermon now turns directly on "the political spectacle" at the turn of the century. A threefold apostasy has taken place—the secularization of the primitive Christian Church, the Reformation, and finally the atheism and materialism of the Age of Enlightenment. The first "guild" consisted of the true priests, the second of the reformed preachers, the last of the enlighteners. In the midst of the darkest night "Europe may awake," if it become a "state of states." The idea of a United States of Europe emerges here. But Novalis pointed out that it is impossible "that secular forces can achieve equilibrium of themselves. A third element alone, secular and at once superterrestrial, can solve this task. No peace can be concluded among the contending powers. All peace is but an illusion, an armed truce." This third element is the ideal of a new Christian communion of the future!

He continues with words bound to affect us most deeply: "Blood will flow over Europe until the day when the nations grow aware of the fearful insanity that drives them in a circle . . . . Religion alone can reawaken Europe and safeguard the nations . . . . Is it true that the nations have laid hold of everything in man—excepting only his heart, his sacred organ?"

With this question the preacher reaches the seventh and last step in his ascent, gaining at the end an enhancement of the beginning. The conquest of nationalism is possible only when the nations discover their heart, when they choose Christ as their leader. What alone can save Europe is not political internationalism but an idealistic cosmopolitanism derived from the spirit of religion. Only in this way can we understand the last section, where Novalis gives a creative metamorphosis of Lessing's threefold idea of the *Education of Mankind*. Threefold is the shape of Christianity—as a religion of joy, as an intermediary bringing faith in redemption, and finally as faith in Christ, his Mother, and the Saints.

In the first part the poet speaks of a threefold apostasy from God, in the second of a threefold heralding of the new Kingdom of God. The first apostasy of the primitive Church was, as it were, a denial of the Holy Ghost. Theological error crept into dogmatic controversy and secularization. The schism of the Reformation was an apostasy from the role of intermediary, the tradition of the Sacrament, the principle of the Son. The abolition of all religion, complete atheism, was a denial of the Father, the true creator of the world.

Man's new ascent retraces these stages in reverse order. The first promise is that of the Father. It uses words taken from the book of Genesis, of the Old Covenant. The second promise speaks of the conception of a new Messiah. The third points to the flame of the Holy Ghost, to the Whitsuntide of a new "world-inspiration."

"It shall come, it must come—the sacred age of everlasting peace," Novalis exclaimed in the style of Lessing's prophetic ideas in the *Education of Mankind*, "when the new Jerusalem shall be the capital of the world." This new Jerusalem is an image directly from the Revelation of St. John. It is neither in Palestine nor in the Papal State in Italy, neither in Germany nor in France. It is not the future capital of the United States of Europe, but the heart of all nations—Christ, the middle of the world, the spirit of the earth.

Christendom or Europe fused the style of the *Hymns* with the admonitory tone of the *Devotional Songs*. One recognizes in it the aphoristic studies, and above all his ideal of "Bible Art." Yet the essay stands as something that cannot be compared with anything that had gone before. It seems to ascend a further step into Novalis' inner world, representing a milestone in a field heretofore untrodden.

A century of brotherhood and tolerance, of cosmopolitanism and reconciliation with the spirit of Christianity—that is what Novalis felt he was proclaiming. His friends in the early Romantic movement were like scouts of a youth movement of the new century. In their circles the full emancipation of women and of the Jews was already an anticipated achievement. Dorothea Veith, Henrietta Herz, and Rachel Levin were fully accepted in these circles, and the beginnings of Mendelssohn and Heine were inseparably bound up with them. The Prussian Junker caste was at this time, the time of the Peace of Basle, remarkably calm and unmilitant.

Novalis was to be spared the sight of all these hopes coming to naught. They turned into their very opposites—fanatical nationalism and chauvinism, reaction and the nationalist student movement, race and class hatred, the triumph of materialism, a pernicious fruit that followed the curse of the Napoleonic Wars. But the true tragedy of his lonely mission lay in the fact that those who were closest to him drew away, deserting their youthful ideals and betraying their own cause. This is the fateful background to the rejection of his essay by the Jena Romanticists.

Seen from without, the incident was trifling. It was but natural that the work of a young writer should be subjected to criticism, the more so since but recently even Goethe and Schiller had had to traverse the purgatory brought upon them by the *Xenien*. There had been no dearth of enthusiastic approval for the *Hymns* prepared for the *Athenaeum,* nor for the *Devotional Songs,* which were compared to Goethe's lyricism. The fact of the rejection of the essay becomes quite intelligible in the light of the deficiencies, contradictions and images of Novalis' "tropic and enigmatic tongue."

Insofar as the essay is a preachment and the preachment expands into a vision, it hovers, as it were, above the area of history, even though it uses historical facts and dates. This vacillation between philosophical study and exalted preachment, historical review and vision into the future, brings out many a contradiction of material expression and mythical image, explaining the bafflement of the critics.

What sealed the fate of the essay at the time was the persistent misunderstanding of its eschatological character as a sermon. He pleaded and prayed as a preacher. Terms such as "the true Catholic faith," "the Pope as the vicar of a visible government on earth," "a spiritual order to bring back an enhanced return of the old order" - to him these were metaphors in his sermon, not concepts in a philosophy of history.

As late as thirty-seven years after the death of Novalis, Tieck stated: "We found these historical views too weak and inadequate, the conclusions drawn too arbitrary." Even Schleiermacher declared in his commentaries on his *Discourses* (1821) that at the time he had opposed Novalis and warned against his essay, for "into what barbarous depths of the unholy past would that return us!" Schelling wrote a satirical poem *Heinz Widerporst*, about a man who turned Catholic, a parody on Novalis, and he intended to publish it in the journal *Athenaeum*. In the end, August Wilhelm Schlegel submitted both *Christendom or Europe* and *Widerporst* to Goethe, who decided against the acceptance of both papers.

Goethe too, in his Fairytale, dealt in revelation. But his "apocalypse" remained wholly within his poetic imagery, and never departed from the sphere of creative art. It is understandable that Goethe felt little enthusiasm for Novalis' preachment. Such "idealized treatment" was alien to him. He rejected it even in Schiller.

Christendom or Europe bears the marks of the former disciple of Schiller. It is in this connection that Novalis wrote that the historian should become an orator since he proffers gospels and all history is gospel. In this sense his essay, too, is a fairytale. One is often reminded of scenes in Klingsor's tale, of the realm of Arcturus, where this new first rally takes place and where we read such words as "let each prepare himself for the birth!"

The pros and cons stirred up by the work are symbolic of the poet's own destiny and at once of that of his friends. A first fissure trembled across the world of the Romanticists. It was not long afterward that their whole covenant was shattered and the flock was dispersed. Within three years not a single one of them was left at Jena. Tieck was the first to go - the very next summer he hastened to Dresden. August Wilhelm Schlegel moved to Berlin. A year later Friedrich and Dorothea Schlegel settled in Paris. Caroline divorced Schlegel and married Schelling with whom she went to Würzburg. . . .

The century that rose out of the gloom of those winter days gave little attention to the world of Novalis. His oration, meant for his own age and his own people, remained unheard, unread, unprinted.

9. HEINRICH VON OFTERDINGEN

The *Fragments* had been like the soliloquies of a collector who learned as he accumulated. *The Novices of Sais* had spoken in dialogue, like a choir of students gathered about their master. The tales had painted rhapsodic stage settings of this choir. *The Hymns to the Night* had sounded forth as the inner self's song and response to Christ and Sophia. The *Devotional Songs* had preached and prayed for the congregation. *Christendom or Europe* had addressed itself to the nations and to the turn of the century. But *Heinrich von Ofterdingen* was composed as the poet's symphony on the mission of poetry. It is the testament the poet bequeathed to us.

In Artern, at the foot of the Kyffhäuser mountain, Novalis was visiting the home of his friend Funk, whose *History of Emperor Frederick II* he was reading. Novalis was also studying the *Chronicles of Thuringia,* Johannes Rothe's *Life of St. Elizabeth,* and Cyriacus Spangenberg's *Chronicles of Mansfeld.*

The so-called *Prose Report of the Wartburg Contest* names a certain Heinrich Afterding who entered the competition in the year 1207, together with five other minstrels - Heinrich the Virtuous Scribe, Walter von der Vogelweide, Reinhart von Zweten, Wolfram von Eschenbach, and Biterolf. Only in Bodmer's edition of the *Minnesingers* is the name Afterding given as Ofterdingen. Described as the only one of the minstrels to take the side of the Duke of Austria, he lost the contest against Walther and the others, who were enlisted on the side of the Landgrave of Thuringia. Ofterdingen invoked the protection of the Landgravine Sophia to fetch the minstrel Klingsor from Hungary. The latter hastened to Wartburg castle, where he put a test of questions to Wolfram. Wolfram answered them all, and in accordance with custom this should have sealed Ofterdingen's fate, sentencing him to death. The Wartburg poem, however, fails to mention him further on, and the circumstances surrounding his end remain obscure.

There is no historical evidence to testify to the existence of a man named Ofterdingen, although he was sometimes considered to be author of the Nibelungen saga. He achieved immortality only in the work of Novalis. Later on Richard Wagner freely recreated him as Thannhäuser, making him a contemporary of Saint Elizabeth.

The external sources of the novel were the *Chronicles of Mansfeld,* compiled in the County where Novalis was born, the legend of the Kyffhäuser mountain and the Blue Flower, part and parcel of the oral folklore tradition of the poet's homeland. But what was it that Novalis shaped from his own innermost world? His fragmentary notes reveal that the archmotif of his work was the transfiguration of the mission of poetry, a novel of the poet par excellence - in contrast to Goethe's *Wilhelm Meister's Apprenticeship.* Goethe's famous novel seems like an anvil struck by the hammer of Novalis' creation, kindling a spark.

To the youthful genius of Novalis it was self-evident that he could not function as a mere imitator of Goethe, but rather must build a world of his own to be placed at the side of Goethe. What he expected of Goethe was that he might grow beyond the sensuality of the *Roman Elegies*, the realism of *Wilhelm Meister*, the civic respectability of *Hermann and Dorothea*, that he might continue along the lofty heights his imagination had explored in the Fairytale. After enthusiastic appraisals he later called *Wilhelm Meister* "a satire on poetry and religion...a poetic contrivance sealing the death of the romantic element" and pronounced his verdict of "creative atheism."

But in a far more comprehensive sense than appears from his notes and from passages of his letters, Novalis' novel takes issue with the art of Goethe. The figure of Klingsor is a portrait of Goethe. It is Klingsor who is Heinrich's teacher, initiating him into the art of poetry. It is Klingsor who tells Heinrich the apocalyptical tale of *Eros and Fable.* In Klingsor Ofterdingen encounters the heritage of antiquity, the classical south. He meets Klingsor not in the north, at Wartburg castle, but at Augsburg, in the south, and the remaining notes on the continuation of the novel make his Faustian way to the Hellas of antiquity unequivocally clear. Like Faust, Ofterdingen was to seal a spiritual union with antiquity.

While Novalis was working at his *Ofterdingen* with his challenge to the art of poetry, he anticipated works of Goethe that were then only in the making. Novalis, of course, could have no idea that in these very years Goethe was continuing his Faust, writing his Prologue in Heaven, the Easter Scene, the pact with Mephistopheles, the beginning of the Classical Walpurgis Night and the third act of the second part of Faust, the Helena Scene - works that did not reach the public until many years after Novalis' death. When Novalis wrote "Goethe himself will and must be surpassed - though only as the ancients can be surpassed, in content, in variety, and depth, not really as an artist, or at least but little. . ." he, indeed, had a foreboding of that which a generation later was so wonderfully deepened in *Wilhelm Meister's Wanderings*, of what emerged in the *Orphic Orisons*, of what was revealed in the *West-Eastern Divan* and in the end of *Faust II*.

The composition of *Heinrich von Ofterdingen*, the most musical of all of Novalis' works, seems to lead us by serpentine paths into the heart of an inner world, and thence, in gradual change, outward again. It is composed of two mighty word symphonies. The two parts into which it is divided are called *The Expectation* and *The Fulfillment*. They are related to each other as are preparation and awakening, purification and initiation. While the second part has remained a fragment, the first part is a fully rounded and perfected symphony. The nine chapters of the *Expectation* are introduced by the narration of two dreams and concluded by the tale of *Eros and Fable*. The action takes place between the dream and the tale. How the dream becomes world, and the world in turn an enhanced dream, is told in the several "movements" of the symphony."

The division of the novel is reflected in the two dedication sonnets. The first introduces Heinrich's path away from his "godmother", the Landgravin Sophia, to Klingsor's daughter, Mathilda: "Mit Ahnungen hast du das Kind gepflegt / Und zogst mit ihm durch fabelhafte Auen, / Hast, als das Urbild zartgesinnter Frauen / Des Jünglings Herz zum höchsten Schwung bewegt."

The archetype of woman - the "Eternal Feminine" - becomes his beloved, his Muse, the guardian spirit of his poetry.

We shall return to the second sonnet in the discussion of the second part. The poet had good reasons for placing it at the beginning of his work, for it is intimately related to the basic theme, the slumbering of the "supreme sense" and the gradual awakening that reveals the mystery of the Blue Flower.

This Blue Flower is the alpha and omega of the whole work. The question as to its nature is posed at the start, but the answer can be given only at the end, for *Heinrich von Ofterdingen* records a path of development, a dream of learning. All outward action merely serves as a symbol for inward events. The poet almost completely forewent realistic characterization of persons and places. Merchants and knights appear merely as groups, speak and act as such. The plot is built up from the outside with the utmost simplicity. It lacks all the effects of dramatic intensification or fictional suspense. This is especially noticeable, for example, in the description of Heinrich's first meeting with Mathilda.

"I long to behold the Blue Flower. It is constantly in my mind, and I cannot think and write of anything else." These are the first words of the book. Its content is this persistent "preoccupation with the Blue Flower" - first as a dream, then as a fantasy, as destiny, as mind, and ultimately as a world of higher reality. But even Heinrich's dream is not an ordinary, arbitrary dream. It is a pilgrimage, an event in itself. How else can the following lines be explained: "His feelings had never been so excited. He went through an infinitely variegated life. Then came death, a return again to life; he loved, loved intensely, and was again separated forever from the object of his passion."

The dream ascends in three stages. Following the first experience, Heinrich climbs a mountain, moistens his lips with holy water, immerses himself in a bath and falls asleep. This slumber within the dream thus becomes the "sleep of sleep." Finally, at the third stage he is awakened by "another insight." Only then does he behold the Blue Flower, its petals revealing the shape of a face. Here Heinrich wakes up and exclaims: "It seems to me to have been something more than a mere dream." All this clearly points to an element of inner experience, a gradual process of awakening.

The father at first mocks Heinrich's dream, calling it mere froth, then recalls a dream of his own, dreamed in Rome just before he returned to Augsburg, where he married Heinrich's mother. The dream had dealt with the legend of Emperor Frederic within Kyffhäuser mountain and with that of the Blue Flower - though the father was unable to recall the color of the flower himself. He had been, indeed, unable to see it, but his Roman companion had told him about the miracle flower. Whoever beheld it would see the wonders of the world, would be the happiest of men and also famous, if only on the evening of St John's Day he would come to Kyffhäuser mountain and "devoutly beseech God for the interpretation of this vision."

But the father did not so pray. To him dreams were but castles in the air. Yet he, too, had a sudden insight, for he confessed: "How free was my tongue, and what I spoke sounded like music."

We have said before that the novel has almost symphonic form. The two dreams in the first chapter sound like preludes which set the key of the entire fugue to come. In a sense the father's dream anticipates the main outlines of the first part. It is annunciation, expectation. Heinrich's own dream, on the other hand, points to "The Fulfillment" in the second part.

About the time of St. John's Day, when he took leave of his ancestral city, Heinrich was twenty years of age. His experiences in the novel take up his twenty-first year, when the youth attains his majority, his individuality reaching full freedom. His journey from north to south leads from the dream of the self to the reality of the self.

The merchants who accompany Heinrich and his mother on their journey confess, it is true, that they "have not troubled themselves much with the secrets of the poets," yet they proceed to announce to Heinrich profound views on the nature of poetry:

> The poet fills the internal sanctuary of the mind with new, wonderful, and pleasing thoughts. He knows how to awaken at pleasure the secret powers within us, and by words gives us force to see into an unknown and glorious world. We hear strange words and we yet know their import. The language of the poet exerts a magic power; even ordinary words flow forth in charming melody, and enchant the spellbound listener.

The merchants next tell Heinrich the tale which is a free rendering of the Greek legend of the poet Arion, though the name of the Hellenic bard is never mentioned. In Greek legend Arion appears with many of the features of Orpheus. Undoubtedly, it was this primal Orphic image that moved Novalis to retell the myth himself. Arion was touched with the grace of the gods "who by the strange sound of marvellous instruments aroused the secret life of the woods and the spirits hidden in the trees...who tamed the cruel beasts...who swept even the most lifeless rocks into the steady rhythms of the dance."

The bard of the tale journeys across the sea - a legendary sea of yore, teeming with monsters and portents. The treasure his fame has brought him arouses the greed of the ship's crew. The pirates resolve to hurl the bard into the sea to gain possession of his treasure. He in turn begs to be granted the boon of chanting a last lay. The mariners had stuffed their ears, lest they be moved by the song, and scarcely finishing his chant, the bard hurled himself into the sea. A kindly monster (in the Greek myth a dolphin) carried him to the nearest coast and soon brought the treasure as well. For the pirates quarreled and slew one another, while the ship foundered and sank.

Though he recounts the story of Arion word for word, Novalis gives no name to the bard, for he is concerned only with the primal phenomenon of the true poet of yore: priest, healer, and judge in one person who, like Orpheus, is endowed with the transmuting and harmonizing magic of the word. Thus the little fable is the myth of the poet as such. For that reason Novalis incorporated into his novel of poetry the previously written tale.

Another story, likewise told by the merchants and making up the third chapter, carries on certain themes from the *Novices of Sais*. The King of Atlantis - so begins the tale - was old. Since he had no son, none of his subjects seemed worthy of becoming his daughter's consort and his heir.

One day the Princess came to a remote cottage. An old man lived there with his son, whom he was teaching the Atlantean secrets of nature. She was deeply affected by the son who picked up a precious ruby which had dropped from the necklace of the Princess as she was riding home. The youth, not knowing who she was, returned the stone—a symbol of the heart—to the Princess at her next visit and she in turn placed a gold chain about his neck. Soon the two married secretly and hid from the king. After a year the youth appeared before the king in the guise of an unknown minstrel. There he sang "of the Golden Age of yore, ruled by the twin goddesses of Love and Poetry." It was the song of the return of the Golden Age, when Love and Poetry (Eros and Fable) shall rule. The aged King, deeply moved by the song, asked the minstrel to name some gift he would like, but the youth went on to chant another song when his father appeared on the scene, leading a veiled figure carrying an infant. The young minstrel lifted the veil and the Princess proffered her child to her royal father, who blessed the couple in happy reconciliation.

The tale of Atlantis is like a delicate bridge, leading us to the ideas of Eros and Fable which Klingsor's story glorifies later on. In a fragmentary note Novalis calls Klingsor "king of Atlantis" and, indeed, the Atlantis-tale of the merchant appears as the germinal idea for the fairystory which he tells in the ninth chapter at the end of the first part of the novel.

In the fourth chapter the stories of the knights bring home to Heinrich the significance of the pilgrimage to the Holy Sepulchre. In this connection we read these meaningful words: "The flower of his heart revealed itself now and then in flashes of lightning." Suddenly he hears the sound of a woman's voice raised in song. It is Zulima, the woman from the East, a figure resembling Mignon in "Wilhelm Meister," singing a song of yearning as did Mignon. Heinrich takes pity on Zulima, seeks to rescue her and return her to her home. The "lightning-flashes" in the blossom of his heart give him a foreboding of the Blue Flower, but he cannot yet behold it. Zulima foreshadows Mathilda. But before he can meet Mathilda, his soul must undergo another experience. This is described in the fifth chapter.

Heinrich meets a miner from Eula in Bohemia, a figure that bears resemblance to Werner and Boehme. The treasure-digger initiates him into the mysteries of the earth, outlining an ideal vision of his vocation, which is at once a poetic transfiguration of Novalis' Freiberg period and of his work at the Weissenfels salt works. "Mining must be blessed by God; for there is no art which renders those who are occupied in it happier and nobler, which awakens a deeper faith in divine wisdom and guidance, or which preserves the innocence and childlike simplicity of the heart more freshly." The miner passes through the school of selflessness, and this is what Heinrich is to learn from him: "Nature will never be the exclusive possession of any single individual. In the form of property it becomes a terrible poison . . .thus it undermines secretely the ground of the owner."

The miner is the true lord of the earth, when he approaches it with pure heart, and the earth appears as his bride: "Der ist der Herr der Erde, / Wer ihre Tiefen misst, / Und jeglicher Beschwerde / In ihrem Schoss vergisst. / . . . .Er ist mit ihr verbündet, / Und inniglich vertraut, / Und wird von ihr entzündet, / Als wär sie seine Braut."

But the miner may also become slave to the earth, when he succumbs to the craving for gold. Gold is king among the metals, the sun within the rocks; but to him who lacks selflessness it becomes a demon. Of this the Miner in the novel sings in a second song. This is a song of freedom, freedom acquired by him who selflessly loves gold for its own true nature and does not become a slave to this "king of metals." Those whose spirits are "awake," whose souls are selfless, must drive out the evil spirits with the help of the good, increase the numbers of the free, and ultimately make possible the homeward journey to the bosom of heaven. Then will gold once again be the pure image of the sun within the earth, just as it is the goal of his striving, the Philosopher's stone for the alchemist. That is why "it struck Heinrich that he had somewhere heard that song."

Heinrich listens to the discourses of the merchants and knights, and experiences awe, veneration, and valor. The encounter with Zulima awakens the power of compassion within him. The Miner's songs teach him selflessness and inner freedom. Having undergone all these experiences, Heinrich, in the company of the Miner, may now descend into the depths of the earth and become ever more deeply schooled in the mysteries of nature. Here the narrative assumes altogether the tone of a dream-fantasy, and the passage that follows is among the finest in romantic literature: "Der Mond stand in mildem Glanze über den Hügeln, und liess wunderliche Träume in allen Kreaturen aufsteigen. Selbst wie ein Traum der Sonne, lag er über der in sich gekehrten Traumwelt, und führte die in unzählige Grenzen geteilte Natur in jene fabelhafte Urzeit zurück, wo jeder Keim noch für sich schlummerte, und einsam und unberührt sich vergeblich sehnte, die dunkle Fülle seines unermesslichen Daseins zu entfalten."

Suddenly the voice of a Hermit is heard from inside the mountain. It is the Count of Hohenzollern who has sought refuge there in order to pursue his contemplations undisturbed. He now tutors Heinrich on the meaning of the writing of history, inspiring him with veneration for and faith in the guidance of God and of destiny. He says: "History should only be written by old and pious men... it appears to me necessary that a historian should also be a poet; for poets alone know the art of skillfully combining events. There is more truth in their *Märchen* than in learned chronicles."

In the end the Hermit tells Heinrich that his wife Maria lies buried within the mountain, and that a "divine illumination" has come over him ever since he interred her there. The Hermit, in other words, still feels united with his departed spouse, and it is this experience that he calls divine illumination—a state of mind Heinrich must learn to recognize in the Hermit, since he is subsequently to experience it himself.

Having received this message from the Hermit and having been led into the innermost depths of his own soul, Heinrich is now left to himself. Standing in the bowels of the earth, confronted with the cave of caves, he finds the book in which he discovers "his own form quite discernible among the figures." It is the book of his own life. He beholds the entire panorama of his existence, the past reality, the future potentiality. The book bears no title, for he himself is the book, and the end is not yet. The scope of his future is outlined, but the path of freedom must be of his very own making. The Hermit himself calls the book "a romance... wherein the art of poesy is represented and extolled in all its various relations." Thus it contains the prototype or plan of Novalis' own novel. But since this is the story of Ofterdingen, it is at once the book of his life. It is clear that this book is not a parchment manuscript of the Middle Ages, no more than the Hermit must be interpreted literally when he says that he secured the book in Jerusalem.

Heinrich's reading of this life chronicle lies at the middle point of the first part. It forms the core of all the events on the journey from Eisenach to Augsburg. From the aspect of the novel as a symphony, this passage sounds like the gentle fading of an adagio or andante, the symphonic middle-movement, to be followed by two further movements in more rapid tempo.

The sixth chapter, picturing the arrival in Augsburg, is a scherzo or an allegro. The colorful festival at the house of Heinrich's grandfather, Schwaning, seems to foreshadow the War of the Minstrels. Schwaning sings a graceful love-song, which is followed by Klingsor's drinking-song. Everything in this chapter is attuned to the meeting between Heinrich and Mathilda. Scarcely has Heinrich come to know Klingsor's daughter when he invites her to dance.

Mathilda's face is compared to a "lily inclined toward the rising sun." If we are to see in Klingsor a portrait of Goethe, we must ask ourselves what his daughter, "the spirit of her father in the most lovely disguise," represents. Surely what is meant here is the Beautiful Lily of Goethe's *Fairytale*, which Novalis so deeply admired and sought to interpret. He not only compares Mathilda with Lily, but associates her with the mystery of the Blue Flower. For during the night following the festivities, Heinrich again dreams of the Blue Flower. "What peculiar connection is there between Mathilda and that flower? That face, which bowed toward me from the petals, was Mathilda's heavenly countenance." And now Heinrich remembers having seen the face of Mathilda in the book, as "the visible spirit of song . . . She will dissolve me into music. She will become my inmost soul, the guardian spirit of my holy fire." She is to become his Muse.

But scarcely has he grown aware of this, when his dream brings him the tragic destiny of Orpheus and Eurydice:

> The thoughts of his soul flowed together into wonderful dreams. A deep blue stream glimmered from the green plains. A boat was floating on the smooth surface. Mathilda was sitting in it and steering. She was adorned with garlands, singing a simple song, and looked over toward him with sweet sadness. His bosom was oppressed, he knew not why. The sky was clear; the water quiet. Her heavenly face was reflected in the waves. Suddenly the boat began to whirl. He cried out to her earnestly. She smiled and laid down the helm in the boat which continued its whirling. He was seized with overwhelming fear. He plunged into the stream, but could not move, and was hurried along. She beckoned to him, as if she had something to tell him, and though the boat was fast filling with water, yet she smiled with unspeakable tenderness, and looked down serenely into the whirlpool. Suddenly it drew her in. A gentle breath of air passed over the stream, which flowed on as quiet and glimmering as ever. His intense anxiety robbed Heinrich of all consciousness. His heart no longer throbbed. On recovering his senses, he was on the dry land.

A curious dialogue concludes the dream, promising Heinrich that he shall be reunited with Mathilda in spirit:

" 'Where is the stream?' he cried with tears.

" 'Do you not see its blue waves above us?'

"He looked up, and the blue stream was flowing gently ove his head.

" 'Where are we, dear Mathilda?'

" 'With our fathers.'

" 'Shall we remain together?'

" 'Forever,' she replied, while she pressed her lips to his, an so embraced him that she could not tear herself from him. Sh put a wondrous, secret word into his mouth, and it rang throug his whole being."

Heinrich would have dearly loved to dredge up into his co

sciousness this word that rang through his whole being. But he woke up and had forgotten it. "He would have given his life to remember that word."

The seventh and eighth chapters carry the discourse on poetry and love. Klingsor-Goethe shows Heinrich how reason and feeling must balance each other. True insight into nature is the poet's most indispensable faculty. Inspiration untempered by reason is dangerous. "In every composition chaos should shine through the well-clipped foliage of order." Poets cannot study music and painting enough, for "the execution, not the material, is the object of the art." Poetry, Klingsor concludes his masterly discourse, should really have no name of its own, for "it arises from the peculiar action of the human spirit. . .Love itself is nothing but the highest poetry of nature."

With these words Klingsor leaves Heinrich, saying that Heinrich knew more about the nature of love than did he. What follows now is the final great dialogue between the two lovers. Once again they state Novalis' own message, the quintessence of his doctrine of love. Man is eternal because of his power to love. At bottom, religion is the everlasting union of loving hearts. For wherever two lovers are gathered, the spirit of God dwells within them. "Thy earthly shape is but a shadow" of this ideal image, Heinrich exclaims. "The earthly faculties strive and swell that they may incarnate it; but nature is yet unripe; the form is only an eternal archetype, a fragment of the unknown holy world."

Because nature is yet unripe, it can be brought to mature perfection only through man's love, for "the higher world is nearer to us than we usually believe. Here already we live in it, and we see it closely interwoven with our earthly nature." Love unites the two worlds forever, for "it is truly a most mysterious flowing together of our most secret and personal existence." It is the presence of God within man.

Thus Heinrich's self has found itself in Mathilda. The ego's ego has awakened. He has come of age, in his twenty-first year. His poetic genius has been born. Mathilda is his Muse. This inner union is now to be celebrated on earth. But instead of describing this earthly wedding, Klingsor gives us the powerful images of the tale of Eros and Fable, which conclude the first part, "The Expectation."

At the first glance this part of the novel, like the tale of Eros and Fable, seems to be sketchy and lacking in structure. One is often confused by the inserted stories, which seem to interrupt the flow of the narrative. But likewise, as we have seen in closer examination of the fairy-tale, we are able to discern a definite structure of the entire first part of the novel.

We see seven stages described in chapters two to eight. They are introduced by a narrative of two dreams (in the first chapter) and are concluded by the tale which Klingsor relates in the ninth chapter. From dream to tale there takes place the self-education of Heinrich. In the beginning stand the dreams of Heinrich and his father, at the end the world of Klingsor's fantasy. How the dream becomes world, and the world in turn an enhanced dream - that is told in the several "movements" of the symphony.

In the second and third chapters, Heinrich's mentors on his peregrination are the merchants who prepare him for his future vocation by telling him two tales, those of Arion and Atlantis.

In the fourth chapter the knights bring close the world of the crusades. A meeting with a woman from the East brings Heinrich face to face with the Orient. Zulima is the first person to speak to him individually. The merchants and knights act and talk only as a plurality.

The fifth chapter leads us deeply into the world of individual personality. Heinrich encounters a miner who in turn leads him to a hermit. The hermit leaves Heinrich to himself in the solitary cave, until Heinrich learns to read the book of his own life. Here we are, as it were, at the inmost heart. Then the serpentine way again leads outward.

The sixth chapter describes the end of Heinrich's journey and his arrival in Augsburg where, in the house of his grandfather, he meets Klingsor and his daughter Mathilda.

The seventh and eighth chapters tell us of Heinrich's discipleship and his consecration as poet. He becomes Klingsor's son and Mathilda's suitor. While the earthly wedding is being prepared, Klingsor tells the tale of Eros and Fable, which concludes the first part.

Thus, the first part of the novel is polished down to the last detail, like a symphony with theme and countertheme constructed almost in counterpoint. It should be noted, for example, how the theme in the second and third chapters corresponds to that in the seventh and eighth. Both of these pairs carry over the action in the same place and merge inwardly, one into the other. In the second chapter the tale of Arion heralds the theme of the poet's destiny. In the eighth chapter the promise becomes reality in the love of Mathilda.

In the fourth chapter Heinrich meets Zulima, the woman from the East, like a premonition of the encounter with Mathilda which takes place in the sixth chapter. The knights' songs of the crusades in the fourth chapter have their counterpart in the drinking and love songs at the house of Schwaning in the sixth chapter.

The fifth chapter, heart of the composition, stands entirely by itself. Aside from Klingsor's tale, it is by far the most voluminous chapter. It has no counterpart in the symphonic structure. Its structure is threefold - the miner, the hermit, the book - like concentric circles leading to the heart's own heart.

The theme of the Blue Flower threads its way through the entire work. It is at the center of the dreams in the beginning, it is woven into the action in the middle of the work; in the tale it is linked with the mystery which Sophia seeks to guard in the temple. It is associated with Mathilda's secret word. It is the key that leads us to Heinrich's heart. If we understand it rightly, it will reveal to us the ultimate meaning of Novalis' work as a whole.

10. THE BLUE FLOWER

The second sonnet of the novel *Heinrich von Ofterdingen* tells us: "Ich ward durch sie zu allem, was ich bin, / Und durfte froh mein Angesicht erheben. / Noch schlummerte mein allerhöchster Sinn. / Da sah ich sie als Engel zu mir schweben / Und flog, erwacht, in ihrem Arm dahin. "

The first part of the novel, *The Expectation,* is the hope that this slumbering sense may awake. The second part, *The Fulfillment,* is the awakening of this "highest sense." What is this sense? Since, in contrast to the physical senses, it is yet undeveloped, the poet points to it in symbolic pictures of a gradual revelation. That symbol is the Blue Flower.

From this viewpoint we get a much clearer grasp of Heinrich's words: "I long to behold the Blue Flower. It is constantly in my mind (*Sinn*)." Since it is not the expression of a physical sense (*Sinn*) located in the body, we are told that it begins "to move and change." The dream of the Blue Flower is not about a static object at rest, but about a dynamic process. Hence the poet calls it a "split in the mysterious curtain, which, with a thousand folds, hides our inward natures from our view. . . . hurrying (us) along with it in its mighty revolutions".

In Klingsor's tale (at the end of the first part of the novel) Sophia proclaims: "Within each dwells the heavenly Mother giving birth to every child forevermore. . .feel ye not the sweetest birth in the beating of your heart?" These words carry a key that may serve to open a new door to an understanding of the Blue Flower, once we have examined the fragmentary second part of the novel.

The Blue Flower is revealed as "the sweet birth in the beating of the heart." It is by such a birth that the child Astralis appears. Astralis is the spiritual (astral) child of Heinrich and Mathilda. Since death has torn Mathilda from Heinrich's arms, the marriage contracted on earth is henceforth founded only in the realm of the spirit. This spirit child tells us that it was born on a summer morn, yet it becomes quite clear that this could not have been a birth in the physical sense. Astralis is a being that "awakes" more and more. It says of itself: "Ye know me not, ye saw me yet forming."

Astralis is unknown to us, for it is still an undiscovered being slumbering within us. But we saw Astralis "forming" - in the dreams of Heinrich, in the tales of the novel. In the end Astralis resorts wholly to the symbolic language of the flowers when saying: "Ich duftete, die Blume schwankte still / In goldner Morgenluft. Ein innres Quellen / War ich, ein sanftes Ringen, alles floss / Durch mich und über mich und hob mich leise./ Da sank das erste Stäubchen in die Narbe,/ Denkt an den Kuss nach aufgehobnem Tisch. / Ich quoll in meine eigne Flut zurück -/ Es war ein Blitz - nun konnt ich schon mich regen, / Die zarten Fäden und den Kelch bewegen. . / Nicht einzeln mehr nur Heinrich und Mathilde / Vereinten beide sich zu einem Bilde. / Ich hob mich nun gen Himmel neugeboren, / Vollendet war das irdische Geschick / Im seligen Verklärungsaugenblick."

Since Astralis is a spiritual being, the poet has need of symbols—flowers, inner gushing (*innres Quellen*), gentle striving (*sanftes Ringen*), flash (*Blitz*), swell (*Regung*); fertilization [dust-seeds (*Stäubchen*), shell (*Narbe*), petals (*Fäden*), cup (*Kelch*)], ascent to heaven, rebirth, transfiguration! All these expressions become metaphoric of the awakening of an inner process. Astralis is the herald who proclaims the realm of the Blue Flower as the symbolic expression for an inner attainment: "Es bricht die neue Welt herein / Und verdunkelt den hellsten Sonnenschein, / Man sieht nun aus bemoosten Trümmern / Eine wunderseltsame Zukunft schimmern / . . . .Der Liebe Reich ist aufgetan, / Die Fabel fängt zu spinnen an."

These words hint that the world of fable has become reality, that it is an enhanced dream, and that this dream becomes an enhanced world. Hence the message of the Astralis-child culminates in these words: "The dream is World, the World is Dream."

The dream of the Blue Flower, at the outset of the first part of the novel, becomes the world of the tale told at its very end. The Astralis-child is a "dream become world;" in other words, it is born from the spiritual union between the poet's word (Heinrich) and the pure power of love (Mathilda). Astralis is a child of the realm of the night, an offspring of the supersensible, revealing itself in the sensible world of the day.

At the beginning of the second part we learn that Mathilda did indeed drown in the stream, as foreshadowed in Heinrich's dream. In this sense, too, "dream becomes world." Heinrich now pursues his lonely pilgrimage away from Augsburg. His grief over Mathilda's death is described with such immediacy and beauty of language that we might almost be reading passages from Novalis' own lamentations over Sophia, noted in his diaries three years earlier.

The voice of Mathilda, transfigured, speaks from a tree. Death appears to Heinrich "a high revelation of life." Just as Novalis had become a poet only on the death of Sophia, so Heinrich von Ofterdingen, the pilgrim, only now sings the first song of his own to the lute. It is one of Novalis' most perfect creations, and it was destined to be his last.

After this song, a girl steps to the side of the pilgrim to console him, as Mathilda had promised. We are at once reminded of Julie von Charpentier, to whom Novalis was betrothed after the death of Sophia and whom he intended to marry at the time he wrote the novel. But this biographical aspect is of no significance. For the discourse with the girl whose name, Cyane, reminds us of a flower, sounds a theme that belongs to the realm of the Blue Flower. This is the concept of metempsychosis. Cyane herself appears in a new mortal guise, for she was the late daughter of the Count of Hohenzollern and his wife Maria. Cyane guides Heinrich to the physician Sylvester, who in his former life was host to Heinrich's father at Rome and who then appeared in the father's dream as the guide explaining the nature of the Blue Flower.

The discourse between Heinrich and Cyane is certainly among the most baffling passages in the whole work, and we are entitled to believe that, had the poet had a chance for final revision of the second part, he might have clarified a few obscure and contradictory passages. Cyane tells Heinrich that the Mother of God has told her about him, and she calls the Mother of God her own mother. Later on she names Maria of Hohenzollern as her mother, while her father is also Heinrich's father, for she tells him: "Thou hast more parents." It is clear that we must consider these words in a metaphoric sense. The Mother of God is the archetype of all women, the image that reappears in every woman. In this symbolic sense the Count of Hohenzollern is also Heinrich's "father," for he initiates Heinrich into the meaning of history.

"Whither are we going?" Heinrich asks, and Cyane replies "Ever homeward." The words remind us of the "Fragment" that says that philosophy is the urge to be at home everywhere. Cyane indeed seeks to bring about this philosophical mood before taking Heinrich to the physician Sylvester. Heinrichs discourse with Sylvester attains the lofty intellectual heights of one of Plato's Dialogues. In language and thought it is the most profound piece of the novel, the last words given to Novalis to conceive when death wrested the pen from his hand.

Sylvester now guides Heinrich to an immediate understanding of the Blue Flower, an effort in which his previous earthly incarnation did not succeed in the case of Heinrich's father at Rome. Sylvester's thoughts on education, especially reverence and humble self-denial, strangely anticipate ideas Goethe was to develop decades later in *Wilhelm Meister's Wanderings*. Heinrich gains the conviction "that destiny and mind are but names of one idea." Sylvester then turns the conversation to the world of flowers. Heinrich calls flowers "the counterpart of children" and clouds a second "higher childhood." They come to talk of thunder clouds and lightning, which leads the two to examine conscience. The passage reminds us of the "flower" of Heinrich's heart revealing itself like lightning-flashes, in the fourth chapter of the first part.

Lightning-flashes are but "awakening voices . . . of the higher nature, of divine conscience within us. That which is mortal totters to its base; the immortal grows more serene and recognizes itself." Heinrich asks his friend to make the nature of conscience even clearer to him. Sylvester replies modestly: "Were I God, I could do so; for when we comprehend Conscience, it comes into being." He calls conscience the mystery of the highest indivisible unit, individuality, the germ of all personality. It is from Sylvester's words on conscience that the nature of the Blue Flower is brought home closest to us. These were the last pages Novalis was to write. In beauty of form and depth of thought they seem almost like his testament:

"The Conscience appears in every perfection, in every fashioned truth. Every inclination and ability transformed by reflection into a universal type becomes a phenomenon, a phase of Conscience. All formation tends to that which can only be called Freedom; though by that is not meant an idea, but the creative realm of all being. Such freedom is mastery . . . To speak accurately, this all-embracing freedom . . . is the essence, the impluse of Conscience. In it is revealed the sacred individuality, the immediate creation of Personality, and every action of the master is at once the announcement of the lofty, simple, uncomplicated world—God's word...Conscience is the innate mediator of every man. It takes the place of God upon earth, and is therefore to many the highest and the final judge. But how far was former knowledge, called ethics, from the pure shape of this lofty, comprehensive, personal thought. Conscience is the individual essence of the human race fully glorified, the divine archetype of Man."

To Heinrich conscience appears "like the spirit of the world-poem." The true spirit of fantasy, of poetry, he calls "the spirit of virtue in friendly disguise. . . . As virtue is the indwelling divinity among men, the marvelous reflex of the higher world, so also is fable." Just as Klingsor, through his daughter Mathilda, offered Heinrich the experience of knowing love's highest nature, so Sylvester becomes the preceptor of true virtue, religion.

From the two is born the pure art of poetry. Both, love and religion, are the "flowers" of the supernatural world that help, in a higher sense, to awaken us. This is the final inspirational insight that comes to Heinrich from the innocence of his heart, and that is why Sylvester calls him a prophet - a herald of things to come. Heinrich recognizes in conscience the power which "unites this world with higher worlds." In a loftier sense religion appears "as the presence of God in our truest self."

Here the work breaks off. It is like a symbol of Novalis' own life. For his work was not destined to rest in the wealth of the harvest but to stir in the blessings of germination. It is with reverence rather than with critical curiosity that we ought to look at the hundreds of plans, schemes, and fragmentary thoughts to be found in his notes, of which Tieck wrote that he "could not regard the smallest piece of a shattered picture of Raphael or Coreggio with more reverent sorrow."

This much we do sense: The hints concerning the War of the Minstrels, Heinrich's journey to Rome and Greece, his appearance at the imperial court, his finding of the Blue Flower, his transfiguration - all this would have made small what went before, would have given rise to new works, would have, in the eyes of posterity, rivaled such works as Goethe's *Wilhelm Meister's Wanderings* and scenes from the second part of *Faust*. Let us here but mention a few lines at the end of the notes that have been preserved, for they hint at the central theme of the Blue Flower: St. John the Evangelist guides Heinrich into the Kyffhäuser mountain and talks with him about the Apocalypse. Ultimately they reach a cave where Mathilda lies asleep. There they find Astralis, and while they are talking to the child, Mathilda slowly awakes. The folowing remark comes immediately: "He [Heinrich] is to pick the Blue Flower and bring it hither . . . . He picks the Blue Flower and turns to stone. The woman from the East sacrifices herself at the stone, which turns into a sounding tree. The shepherd girl fells the tree and cremates herself together with it. He [Heinrich] turns into a golden ram. . . . Mathilda has to sacrifice him. He becomes Man."

The picking of the Blue Flower thus is not the attainment of a treasure, but the experience of change into a higher order of man. This change is the birth of the perfect man. It retraces symbolically the whole genesis of nature from stone through plant to animal. That mythical events are here portrayed becomes clear from such designations as "sounding tree" and "golden ram."

The Blue Flower of the legend bears the same relationship to the theme of the novel as the figure of Ofterdingen in the legend of the War of the Minstrels to the novel's hero. Both in the legend and the novel, Ofterdingen is a poet, and so, too, the basic character of the Blue Flower is preserved in both. Whoever possesses it attains happiness and wisdom. In the legendary sense, however, happiness and wisdom do not mean wealth and learning, but rather true humanity. The picking of the Blue Flower is the symbolic expression for the awakening of a sense. As the Blue Flower lies hidden inside the mountain, the power to animate a higher sense slumbers within the heart of man. It is a manifest secret - manifest because it dwells within curselves. Yet it is a secret because it must first be lifted from the depths of our nature.

Hence we may say: The Blue Flower awakens the sense which demands the progress of mankind. "To augment the senses and to perfect them" is part of the chief task of the development of the human race and its gradual elevation, reads a fragmentary aphorism, and another says: "Nature cannot be declared moral by standing still but only by progressing . . . . we perceive God but by the moral sense. The moral sense is the sense of existence. . . the sense of the highest - the sense of harmony." And again: "All sense is symbolic - a medium."

Such a symbol of a medium as an organ of supersensible knowledge is the Blue Flower. It is the fundamental motif of all writings of Novalis. "The word symbol is symbolic in itself," he wrote once. Thus, using its own image metaphorically, we might describe the rôle of the Blue Flower in Novalis' works as follows: The motif of the Blue Flower slumbers as a *seed* within the early writings of the fragmentary thought: it *blossoms* within the tales, hymns and songs, and it ultimately *matures as fruit* in *Heinrich von Ofterdingen*.

In philosophical terms Novalis, the student of Fichte, had said in *Blütenstaub* that man may "consciously transcend his senses . . . . The more our senses grow refined, the better able do they become to distinguish individuals. The highest sense would imply the capacity to perceive the completely unique" - in other words, the nature of the individual self.

It is in this connection that he conceived the poetic symbol of the lifting of the veil in the tale of Hyacinth and Rosebud in the *Novices of Sais*. In the tale of Atlantis he speaks of "the heart's own heart" as the cntral organ to perceive our "unique nature," the inner self. "To stir the sacred sense of intuition. . . to animate the life of the heart" - such are the purposes of the *Devotional Songs*. In the essay *Christendom or Europe*, the theme reappears as the "immortal sense of the invisible," that can never be destroyed, though ill winds may "dim and paralyze it, crowd it out with other senses." It is the "sacred sense" that must again rise. In Klingsor's tale Sophia proclaims it as the great mystery "manifest to all, yet ever unfathomable."

Ofterdingen is supposed to find the Blue Flower in its stage of ultimate maturity. His finding and picking of the Blue Flower leads him to the holy union with his higher self. Freedom is the essence of conscience, the innate mediator of God's word. Love is God's own presence within us. Thus the ultimate aim of man is to become the living spirit of freedom and love.

I. Editions of Novalis' Works
in the English language

Henry of Ofterdingen, J. Owen, Cambridge, Mass., 1842. 2nd edition, H. H. Moore, New York, 1853.

Christianity or Europe, London, 1844.

Hymns and *Thoughts on Religion,* Edinburgh, 1888.

Novalis, His Life, Thoughts and Works, ed. and transl. by M. J. Hope, A. C. McClurg, Chicago, 1891.

Devotional Songs, German and English, ed. by B. Pick, Chicago, 1910.

Hymns to the Night, Warner's Library of the World's Best Literature, Vol. 18, or 27, pp. 10724-10732.

English translation of "Hyacinth and Rosebud," portions of the first two "Hymns to the Night," one of the "Devotional Songs," one "Song of Mary," and a few aphorisms, in K. Francke *The German Classics,* New York, 1913-1914, vol. 4, pp. 180-191.

Novalis, Fragments, translated by Thomas Carlyle and by M. J. Hope, reprinted in *Twice A Year,* Vol. XIV-XV, Winter 1946-47, New York, 1946, pp. 181-187.

Hymns to the Night, transl. by Mabel Cotterell, with an introduction and appreciation by August Closs, Bristol University, Phoenix Press, London, 1948.

The Novices of Sais, transl. by Ralph Manheim, with an introduction by Stephen Spender and sixty drawings by Paul Klee, Curt Valentin, New York, 1949.

II. Essays and Studies
about Novalis and his Age
published in the United States and Great Britain.*

Carlyle, Thomas, *Novalis, Essays on the Greater German Poets and Writers,* 1829.

---

* In chronological order.

Later in *Critical and Miscellaneous Essays*, Boston, 1835, 2nd edition 1860.

Curwen, Henry, *Sorrow and Song*. Studies of literary struggle, (Balzac, Hardenberg, Murger, Petöfi, Poe) London, 1875.

Japp, Alexander H., "Friedrich von Hardenberg (Novalis)," *German Life and Literature*, London, 1878.

Boyesen, H. H., *Essays on German Literature*, "Novalis and the blue flower," London, 1892.

Francke, Kuno, "The social aspects of early German Romanticism," *Publications of the Modern Language Association*, Vol. X, New York, 1895.

Wernaer, Robert M., *Romanticism and the Romantic School in Germany*, New York, 1910.

Haussmann, J. F., "Die deutsche Kritik über Novalis 1800-1900," *Modern Philology*, Vol. 9, 1912/13.

Haussmann, J. F., "Die deutsche Kritik über Novalis 1850-1900," *Journal of English and Germanic Philology*, Vol. XII, Urbana, Illinois, 1913.

Porterfield, Allen W., *An Outline of German Romanticism (1766-1866)*, New York, 1914.

Spring, Powell, *The Religion of Novalis*, Wooster, Ohio, 1921.

Heuser, F. W., "Gerhart Hauptmann und Novalis," *The Germanic Review*, Vol. I, New York, 1926.

Silz, Walter, *Early German Romanticism. Its founders and Heinrich von Kleist*, Harvard University Press, Cambridge, Mass., 1929.

Harrold, Charles Frederick, "Carlyle and Novalis," *Studies in Philology*, Chapel Hill, 1930.

Willoughby, L. A., *The Romantic Movement in Germany*, Oxford University Press, London, 1930.

Hofacker, Erich, "Novalis und Christian Morgenstern," *The Germanic Review*, Vol. VI, October, 1931.

Rose, W., *Men, Myths, and Movements in German Literature*, New York, 1931.

Diez, Max, "Metaphor und Märchengestalt III, Novalis und das allegorische Märchen," *Publications of the Modern Language Association*, June, 1933, Vol. XLVIII, No. 2, New York, 1933.

Shine, Hill, "Carlyle and the German Philosophy Problem during the year 1826-27," *Publications of the Modern Language Assocation*, Vol. L, No. 3, September 1935, New York, 1935.

Zeydel, Edwin H., *Ludwig Tieck, The German Romanticist*, Princeton University Press, Princeton, 1935.

Zeydel Edwin H., Percy Matenko and Robert H. Fife: *Letters of Ludwig Tieck* (hitherto unpublished), New York, 1937.

Wagner, Elizabeth, *The scientific interest of Friedrich von Hardenberg* (Novalis), Dissertation, University of Michigan, Ann Arbor, 1937.

Peacock, Ronald, *Hölderlin*, London, 1938.

Peacock, Ronald, "The Poetry of Novalis", *German Studies*, presented to H. G. Fiedler, pp. 323-344, Oxford University Press, London, 1938.

Gode von Aesch, A. G. F., *Natural Science in German Romanticism*, Dissertation, Columbia University, New York, 1941.

Brandt, Richard B., *The Philosophy of Schleiermacher*, New York, 1941.

Spring, Powell, *Novalis, Pioneer of the Spirit*, Winter Park, Florida, 1946.

Hiebel, Frederick, "Novalis", *Twice A Year*, Vol. XIV-XV, Winter 1946-47, pp. 178-180, New York, 1946.

Matenko, Percy, "Fragments from Longfellow's Workshop: Novalis," *The Germanic Review*, Vol. XXII, No. 1, New York, 1947.

Hiebel, Frederick, "Novalis and the Problem of Romanticism," *Monatshefte für deutschen Unterricht*, University of Wisconsin, Vol. XXXIX, No. 8, 1947.

Hewett-Thayer, Harvey W., *Hoffmann, Author of the Tales*, Princeton University Press, Princeton, 1948.

Rehder, Helmut, "Novalis and Shakespeare", *Publications of the Modern Language Association*, Vol. LXIII, No. 2, New York, 1948.

Hiebel, Frederick, "Goethe's Märchen in the Light of Novalis", *Publications of the Modern Language Association*, Vol. LXIII, No. 3, New York, 1948.

Spender, Stephen, "Friedrich von Hardenberg", preface to the *Novices of Sais*, C. Valentin, New York, 1949.

Hiebel, Frederick, "Zur Interpretation der blauen Blume des Novalis," *Monatshefte für deutschen Unterricht*, University of Wisconsin, Vol. XLIII, No. 7, 1951.

INDEX

Names of Persons and Places

A.

Abydos, 55.
Adam, 81.
Aeneas, 22.
Aeschylus, 10.
Aetius, 35.
Afterding, Heinrich, 99.
America, 2, 7, 35.
Apollo, 14, 21, 43, 72.
Apuleius, 67.
Arcturus, 59-65, 68, 98.
Arion, 103, 104, 110, 111.
Ariosto, 10.
Arnold, Gottfried, 51.
Artern, 34, 35, 99.
Atlantis, 57, 104-105, 110.
Augsburg, 100, 102, 107, 110, 113.
August, Prince of Gotha, 49.

B.

Beatrice Portinari, 21, 22, 23, 28.
Beethoven, Ludwig van, 2.
Berlin, 86, 94, 98.
Bethlehem, Pennsylvania, 7.
Biterolf, 99.
Bodmer, Johann Jakob, 99.
Boehme, Jakob, 31, 33, 45, 51, 92, 105.
Boeotes, 61.
Böttiger, Karl August, 27.
Boyeson, H. H., 120.
Brachmann, Christian, 10.
Brandt, Richard B., 121.
Bülow, Eduard von, 1.
Bürger, Gottfried August, 2, 9, 17

C.

Calliope, 21.
Carlowitz, Hans Georg von, 36.
Carlyle, Thomas, 3, 49, 119, 120, 121.
Cerberus, 22
Ceres, 55.
Cervantes, 8.
Charon, 22.
Charpentier, Johann Friedrich Wilhelm von, 28.
Charpentier, Julie von, 23, 28, 29, 31, 34, 35, 113.
Christ, 3, 23, 27, 40, 65, 66, 70-77, 79-82, 84, 86, 90, 91, 93, 95, 96, 99.
Closs, August, 119.
Coleridge, 4.

Constantinople, 35.
Constantine, 35.
Correggio, Antonio, 116.
Cotterell, Mabel, 119.
Curwen, Henry, 120.

D.

Danscour, Jeanette, 18, 19, 20.
Dante Aligrieri, 3, 21, 22, 23, 28, 60, 62.
Danton, George Jacques, 88.
Delphi, 43.
Demeter, 55.
Diez, Max, 121.
Dilthey, Wilhelm, 4, 86.
Dionysus, 14, 43, 55.
Dresden, 27, 34, 35, 36, 58, 98.
Dumas, Charles Guillaume Frederic, 39.
Dürer, Albrecht, 2.
Dürrenberg, 34.

E.

Eisenach, 107.
Eisleben, 10, 11, 15.
Eleusis, 16, 20, 31.
Elijah, 12.
Elizabeth, St., 99.
Empedocles, 35.
Erfurt, 7, 12, 41.
Ernst, Charlotte, 27, 36.
Eros, 59-66, 100, 101, 104, 109, 110.
Erzgebirge, 44.
Eula, 105.
Euripides, 10.
Eurydice, 18, 21, 22, 73, 108.

F.

Faust, 64, 100, 101, 116.
Fichte, Johann Gottlieb, 2, 23, 26, 30, 33, 39, 49, 50, 51, 69, 117.
Fife, R. H., 121.
Florence, 30, 35.
Francke, Kuno, 119, 120.
Frankfurt on the Main, 43.
Franklin, Benjamin, 2.
Freiberg, 27-30, 32-34, 46, 55, 58, 67, 105.
Freya, 59-62, 64, 66.
Frederick II (Hohenstaufen), 99, 102.
Funk, Carl Wilhelm Ferdinand von, 99.

INDEX

G.

Galvani, 29.
Gemma Donati, 23.
Giebichenstein, 34.
Ginnistan, 59-61, 63, 65, 66.
Gioacchino da Fiore, 89.
Gleim, Johann Wilhelm Ludwig, 17.
Gode von Aesch, A. G. F., 121.
Goldacker, Jette von, 20.
Gotha, 7.
Görlitz, 45.
Goethe, Johann Wolfgang von, 2, 3, 8, 15, 23, 24, 27, 29, 30, 34, 41-49, 50, 51, 52, 55, 56, 58, 59, 62, 67, 86, 88, 97, 98, 100, 107, 109, 114, 116, 122.
Göschen, 41.
Göttingen, 8.
Gries, Johann Diedrich, 27.
Grillparzer, Franz, 4.
Grüningen, 18, 20, 21, 24, 26, 28.

H.

Hades, 22.
Halle, 34.
Hardenberg, Anton von, 7.
Hardenberg, Auguste Bernhardine von, 6, 8.
Hardenberg, Bernhard von, 36.
Hardenberg, Carl von, 36.
Hardenberg, Erasmus von, 7, 9, 13, 15, 16, 18, 23.
Hadenberg, Friedrich Wilhelm von, 8, 9.
Hardenberg, Heinrich Ulrich Erasmus von, 5-9, 11-13, 15, 16.
Harrold, Charles Frederick, 120.
Harz, 44.
Haydn, Joseph, 2.
Haussmann, J. F., 120.
Hebbel, Friedrich, 4.
Hegel, Georg Wilhelm Friedrich, 2.
Heimbach, Georg Ludwig August, 9.
Heine, Heinrich, 4, 97.
Heinrich, the Virtuous Scribe, 99.
Hemsterhuis, Franz, 2, 14, 29, 33, 39.
Herder, Johann Gottfried, 2, 35, 43, 51, 87, 89.
Herrnhut, 8.
Herz, Henrietta, 97.
Hesiod, 22.
Heuser, F. W., 120.
Hewett-Thayer, Harvey W., 121.
Hiebel, Frederick, 121, 122.
Hofacker, Erich, 120.
Hoffman, E. T. A., 121.
Hohenelba, 35.
Hölderlin, Friedrich, 2, 10, 24, 37, 121.
Hölty, Ludwig Heinrich Christoph, 17.
Homer, 22, 23.
Hope, M. J., 3, 119.
Horace, 10, 11, 22.
Huch, Ricarda, 4.
Hülsen, August Ludwig, 27.

I.

Isis, 55, 57.

J.

Jacchus, 55.
Jani, Augusta, 19.
Jani, David Christian, 10.
Japp, Alexander H., 120.
Jehova, 80.
Jena, 2, 11, 12, 19, 21, 23, 30, 31, 33, 87, 88, 97, 98.
Jerusalem, 35, 72, 90, 96, 107.
John, the Evangelist, 2, 49, 72, 96, 102, 103, 116.
John, the Baptist, 82.
Julian, the Apostate, 35.
Jung, C. G., 66.
Just, August Cölestin, 4, 18, 35, 36, 51, 64.
Just, Caroline, 68.

K.

Kant, Immanuel, 2, 11, 14, 38, 39, 44, 49, 50.
Klee, Paul, 58, 119.
Kleist, Heinrich von, 24, 37, 120.
Klettenberg, Susanne von, 43.
Klingsor from Hungary, 59, 67, 68, 73, 76, 83, 85, 98, 99, 100, 101, 104, 107, 109, 110, 111, 112, 115, 118.
Klopstock, Friedrich Gottlieb, 17.
Kluckhohn, Paul, 4.
Kösen, 34.
Körner, Christian Gottfried, 27.
Kühn, Sophia von, 18-29, 33, 36, 38, 39, 44, 52, 59, 60-68, 70, 71, 75, 76, 81, 86, 88, 99, 111, 113, 118.
Kyffhäuser Mountain, 34, 35, 99, 102, 116.

L.

Langendorf, 9.
Laube, Heinrich, 4.
Lavater, Johann Kaspar, 43.
Lavoisier, Antoine Laurent, 2, 29.
Lazarus, 72.
Leipzig, 4, 10, 12, 13, 15-18, 24, 27, 34, 40, 41, 43, 88.

INDEX

Lessing, Gotthold Ephraim, 8, 39, 51, 89, 90, 95, 96.
Levin, Rahel, 97.
London, 7.
Longfellow, H. W., 121.
Lucklum, Brunswick, 8, 9, 15.
Louis XVI, 88.
Luther, Martin, 16, 78, 91.

M.

Maeterlinck, Maurice, 4.
Manheim, Ralph, 119.
Mansfeld, 99.
Marat, Jean Paul, 88.
Marie Antoinette, 88.
Mary, 84-86, 90, 96, 114.
Mary Magdalene, 82.
Matenko, Percy, 121.
Matthisson, Friedrich, 17.
Memphis, 55.
Mendelssohn, Felix von, 97.
Mendelssohn, Henrietta, 33.
Mephistopheles, 14, 64, 100.
Michael, Archangel, 66.
Miltitz, Dietrich von, 27.
Minor, Jacob, 4.
Mozart, Wolfgang Amadeus, 2.
Munich, 2.

N.

Napoleon, 2, 88.
Neudietendorf, 7, 8, 9.
Noah, 93.
Nörten, 1, 5.
Nuremberg, 2.

O.

Oberwiederstedt, 1, 5-9.
Orpheus, 18, 21, 22, 29, 72, 73, 103, 104, 108.
Ovid, 22.
Owen, J., 119.

P.

Paracelsus, 35.
Paris, 88, 98.
Pascal, Blaise, 4.
Peacock, Ronald, 121.
Penelope, 22.
Persephone, 22.
Perseus, 59, 60, 64.
Petrarca, 10.
Pick, B., 119.
Pindar, 10.
Pius VI, 88.
Plato, 13, 29, 52, 55, 57, 114.
Plotinus, 29, 55.

Porterfield Allen W. 120.
Priestley, 2.
Prometheus, 35.
Psyche, 73.

R.

Raphael, 31, 32, 58, 116.
Rehder, Helmut, 122.
Reichardt, Johann Friedrich, 2, 34.
Reinhart von Zweten, 99.
Reinhold, Karl Leonhard, 11, 12, 13, 17.
Richter, Jean Paul Friedrich, 27, 34, 35.
Ritter, Johann Wilhelm, 2, 29, 30.
Robespierre, Maximilien François, 88.
Rockenthien, Johann Rudolf von, 18, 20, 25.
Rome, 31, 32, 90, 91, 102, 114, 116.
Rose, W., 120.
Rothe, Johannes 99.
Rudolstadt, 12.

S

Sakuntala, 21.
Samuel, Richard, 4.
Saint Martin, Claude de, 2, 33.
Sappho, 35.
Saturn, 35.
Schelling, Friedrich Wilhelm Joseph, 2, 16, 27, 29, 30, 31, 32, 33, 98.
Schiller, Friedrich, 2, 11, 12, 13, 17, 27, 39-41, 46, 51, 56, 57, 58, 77, 87, 88, 89, 97, 98.
Schlegel, August Wilhelm, 2, 13, 17, 24, 27, 30, 34, 36, 46, 98.
Schlegel, Caroline, 2, 28, 30, 33, 98.
Schlegel, Dorothea, 2, 30, 33, 97, 98.
Schlegel, Friedrich, 1, 2, 13, 14, 15, 17, 18, 24-32, 35, 36, 47, 65, 74, 78, 86, 87, 98.
Schleiermacher, Friedrich, 2, 3, 32, 84, 86, 89, 90, 94, 97, 121.
Schlöben, 9.
Schubert, Franz, 81.
Schubert, Gotthilf Heinrich von, 30.
Severin, Friedrich, 10.
Shakespeare, 2, 8, 24, 25, 26, 122.
Shine, Hill, 121.
Siebeneichen near Meissen, 27, 34.
Silz, Walter, 120.
Simon, Richard, 39.
Solon, 55.
Sophia, Landgravine of Thuringia, 99, 101.
Spangenberg, Cyriacus, 99.
Spener, Philipp Jakob, 6.

Spender, Stephen, 58, 119, 122.
Spinoza, 3, 29, 55.
Spring, Powell, 120, 121.
Stallknecht, F. S., 3.
Starke, Johann Christian, 21.
Steffens, Henrik, 2, 30, 33.

T.

Tennstedt, 17, 26, 39, 88.
Teplitz, 27.
Thannhäuser, 99.
Theocritus, 10.
Thomas Aquinas, 23.
Thümmel, Wilhelmine von, 19.
Tieck, Ludwig, 1, 2, 6, 30-35, 46, 78, 81, 87, 97, 98, 116, 121.
Tolentino, 88.

U.

Upper Lusatia, 34.

V

Valmy, 88.
Virgil, 10, 11, 22, 23.
Voltaire, 49.

W

Wackenroder, Wilhelm Heinrich, 2, 31.
Wagner, Elizabeth L., 121.
Wagner, Richard, 99.
Waller, Friedrich, 87.
Walther von der Vogelweide, 99.
Wartburg, 99, 100.
Weimar, 27, 30, 35, 45, 47.
Weissenfels, 9, 10, 12, 15, 17, 19, 27, 28, 30, 34, 35, 105.
Wernaer, R. M., 120.
Werner, Abraham Gottlob, 27, 29, 55, 58, 105.
Wesley, Charles, 7.
Wieland, Christoph Martin, 2, 8, 9, 12, 17.
Willoughby, L. A., 120.
Wittenberg, 16, 17, 19, 89.
Wolfram von Eschenbach, 99.
Woltmann, Karl Ludwig von, 24.
Würzburg, 98.

Y.

Young, Edward, 9, 77.

Z.

Zeydel, Edwin H., 121.
Zinzendorf, Nikolaus Graf von, 6, 7, 51, 92.

www.ingramcontent.com/pod-product-compliance
Lightning Source LLC
Chambersburg PA
CBHW031316150426
43191CB00005B/261